How to

Piss Off

God

———

How to
Piss Off
God

and the
Long Journey Home

ECHO
Encountering Christ
Helping Others

ECHO PRESS
MICHIGAN, USA

Echo Press
Michigan, USA

Published 2019

ISBN: 978-0-9992887-9-5

Printed in the United States of America

All proceeds will be donated to Echo Missions: www.Echo.love

INTRODUCTION

YOU ARE PROBABLY WONDERING, "HOW DID HE COME up with a title like that?" Unfortunately, you will not learn the answer early on. However, I assure you this: piss off God is exactly what I thought I had done. In fact, I could use much stronger language, but that would be unnecessary and unproductive. The reality is, I had an encounter in the physical realm that science, technology, mysticism, CGI or any other term you can think of does not begin to explain. Ultimately it will be up to you, the reader, to determine if I am full of crap or if it is possible that our reality is just a shroud for the true, unseen existence.

The circumstance I am referring to lasted forty-two minutes. It was July 18, 2015. The time was 11:06 a.m. to 11:48 a.m. To say that it changed the direction of my life would be an extreme understatement. It was more of a transformation. I found myself wrapped in a cocoon of self, unable to see beyond my own world. Everything I did was ultimately to serve myself or my immediate family. Only the power of the light of Jesus could shatter my personal cocoon and show me the darkness that surrounded me. Why in the world He would pursue me after I had demonstrated years of ungodly, self-righteous and arrogant behavior is beyond human understanding. The only logical conclusion I can come up with is that God does not exist in time. He was fully aware that someday the self-serving, self-centered person I was would be guided to become someone different.

This experience I am referring to remains a pinnacle event in my life. The cascade effect that it initiated completely changed the paradigm of my understanding. Unfortunately, I did not pick up on the many earlier signs that should have drawn my attention. Several other situations had occurred in the previous thirty-plus years. Had I been an astute student of spiritual understanding, I may have found certain shortcuts. When a person is strong-willed, self-confident and full of himself, it is hard to break through all these layers.

Pushing the rewind button of my life is imperative. The culmination of all the events from the past three decades would either convince me or leave me as a skeptic. The transparency that I will be sharing comes from the heart of someone who no longer cares what humanity thinks of him. These things that I have written regarding my many failures are by no means justification. Only the knowledge of God can count the number of times that I have done wrong things, said wrong things, and acted inappropriately. If somehow I were ever offered the opportunity to change all these mistakes, I would quickly do so. God can take any experience we have and use it for His glory.

I never imagined I would come to the point of talking about God and how my personal relationship with Jesus is the most important aspect of my life. Because I was in the driver's seat of my life for many years, the importance of such a relationship seemed old-fashioned and unnecessary. Many times I have heard that religion is just a crutch, that at most, it is fire insurance to keep one safe from the gates of hell. This is such a shallow and Satan-driven understanding. The enemy will do anything to get us sidetracked and keep us sidetracked. Often, I would proclaim the blessings of God on my life. That may have been the case initially, but it was really Satan granting me things of this world. He will continue to do that until someone is so deep into the deception that it is nearly impossible to see the light of God.

God knocked on the door of my heart nearly twenty-five years ago. He showed me an opportunity to follow him and what could happen when my wife and I were able to have a God-ordained experience involving the healing of a twelve-year-old brain tumor patient. Unfortunately, about that same time, my then-struggling business began to rapidly change direction. That was when the deception of the enemy came to me disguised as success. Remember, Satan is the god of this world. Many of those in the music and entertainment industry freely admit to selling their souls to the devil. I believe those are outward and conscious decisions that they make. In return, they are granted unbelievable success.

Without a doubt, God blesses us. My business success could have been a blessing from God, but my actions and their results definitely were not pleasing to God. I never made an outward contract with the devil for success, although he slowly slithered his way into my life so that my actions netted no positive gain for the kingdom of God. It was destructive, and I had masqueraded as a Christian for much of my life without any real substance. That is the case with most Christians today. I am not speaking in a voice of condemnation toward others, because I went through it myself. It was simply the life that I was living.

The starting point for this journey is the death of my brother, in 1980. I hope that by sharing the many mistakes in my life I can help those who choose to travel this journey with me gain a deeper understanding. God is patient and kind, and His love endures forever. My desire is that by pointing out the many signs I missed, I can help you see more clearly. I know that God can redeem the time that I have squandered, however, my heart's desire is that I could have enjoyed the closer walk with God much sooner.

CHAPTER 1

———

I GRADUATED HIGH SCHOOL A SEMESTER EARLY, IN 1976, and enrolled at the local community college. During my high school years, I was not particularly popular or unpopular. The fact that I was the only student who got out early and began to attend college probably fueled my arrogance. When I returned to my high school for the graduation ceremony, it seemed as though I had been gone for a couple years. Hanging out with the college kids and going to parties gave me a false sense of maturity over my classmates. I would attend college classes in the evening and work as an auto mechanic during the day. Mechanical skills came easily to me, but I always felt as though I was a second-class citizen as a grease monkey or shop rat.

With the college kids I had access to drugs and alcohol. The money that I made as a mechanic was considerable for the time. I was able to purchase a new car before any of my peers did. Of course, I used the car as a tool to get others to focus their attention on me. A new car made it easy to impress the girls, which in turn resulted in numerous sexual encounters. I was one of those guys who fathers should always warn their daughters about. Anything I could say to get a girl to have sex with me was not off limits. This fed my arrogance, as I was able to smooth-talk my way in and out of most situations. I am ashamed of this, and I warn my own daughter to be aware of those who use flattery. This deceitful behavior is near the top of the list of things I wish I could change.

Unfortunately, many young men are caught in the same trap that I was. Their lives become centered on the next endorphin kick. Through drugs, alcohol, sex and now the blight of pornography propagated by the Internet, hearts and minds are being corrupted at staggering rates. *Proverbs 9:10 NKJV: "The fear of the Lord is the beginning of wisdom, and the knowledge of the holy one is understanding."* This is where understanding the fear of God and the ramifications of our actions need to be emphasized. *Ephesians 6:12 NKJV: "For we do not wrestle against flesh and blood, but against principalities, against powers, against the rulers of darkness of this age, against spiritual host of wickedness in the heavenly places."* Satan has created such a self-serving, self-edifying and self-indulging society that even the popular pictures are called selfies. We look at many of these things as harmless activities. The reality is that they are desensitizing methods that gradually tear down our spiritual defenses. There is one thing about the enemy that should cause great concern for all of us. He is ruthless and patient and has been watching us our entire lives for weaknesses. *1 Peter 5:8 NKJV: "Be sober, be vigilant; because your adversary the devil walks about like a roaring lion, seeking whom he may devour."* Ten years to destroy you is a very small amount of time for him. He loves to have success in your personal destruction and separation from God.

Most weekends, I would spend my time drinking, doing drugs and having sex. All the people I hung out with did the same. My family no longer required me to attend church, and I never really had a relationship with Jesus anyway. Church was something that we did on Sundays and never talked much about during the week. We had prayers before our meals, and that seemed to be the extent of our spiritual enrichment, but my parents always seemed to demonstrate Jesus-like characteristics. My mother, in particular, was a saint. Not only did she have six kids of her own, but she adopted two more, and took care of twenty-six foster children. She was a walking embodiment of a selfless person. I probably was unaware of how her character seeped into mine over the years—a slow drip; I imagine one drop at a time.

I moved out of my parents' house after I graduated. Having my own apartment only enhanced my self-serving lifestyle. Drunken parties and weekends getting high and laid became the norm. It was an empty and shallow existence. I was constantly chasing the self-gratifying prize that always disappeared once obtained. *1 John 2:15 NKJV: "Do not love the world or the things in the world. If anyone loves the world, the love of the father is not in him."* I did not know at the time that there was only one thing to fill that void in me, so the vicious cycle would start over once again. Weekend after weekend merged together into an endless party scene. At the time, it seemed fulfilling and exciting. Now I look back and realize what a waste of life it really was. This behavior continued for many years, but in 1980, life intervened.

My brother, who was one year and three days older than

I was, was killed when the semi he was driving was struck by a train. A malfunction in the train track signal light was blamed for the crash. He was married and going through a divorce. His young son was less than two years old, and it was a very tough time for my parents. On top of that, the Lutheran minister who presided over my family's church refused to do the burial. Pastor Bloom was a haughty and self-righteous chain-smoker. He declared my brother unfit for burial services because he did not attend church on a regular basis. My parents were devastated. Needless to say, they never again attended the church.

I do not believe that this incident caused me to have any negative feelings toward God Himself; they were toward the pastor. Our family found it difficult to talk about our brother; my parents seldom mentioned him. The gloom was like low-lying fog that encased everything in sight.

I had started seeing a girl on a more regular basis at this time. When we went to parties together, I would continue to flirt with other girls. I would exchange physical contact with some as we passed by each other. Usually, these were girls who I had already slept with. The girl I was getting more serious with remained oblivious to this behavior. I am not sure when I fully realized what true love was, but it was not until years into my second marriage that I began to understand. The reason I say this is that I proposed to the girl who I was seeing, even though I was not anywhere near ready to make a commitment.

For some reason, I thought by getting married I could pull my family out of the murky depths of mourning. It was probably one of the worst reasons ever for marrying someone. I continued to see other women after our marriage. I was an unfaithful husband not worthy of the commitment that my first wife had made to me. But something happened to her: She met another guy. This other guy was Jesus, and her commitment to Him steadily grew. She endured my verbal assaults and parading around other girls in front of her. The long suffering that she endured for me was amazing. Clearly, I was an unfit husband and a despicable individual. Many times, she would try to tell me about Jesus, and I could not have cared less. I do not believe I ever considered our marriage seriously, and I had very little, if any, remorse for my actions.

The most incredible thing was that we shared in the birth of a beloved son. I can say with one-hundred percent certainty that I always loved my son. In the worst way, she wanted us to stay together as a family. If I had the relationship with Jesus that I do now, divorce would have never been an option. My first wife and her friends spent countless hours praying for me. Most likely, those prayers stirred something in my soul, but it was not enough to distract me from my selfish desires. After a few failed attempts at saving the marriage, I decided it was time to move on.

The pattern of buying new vehicles to impress people, particularly women, continued unabated. Often, I would get a new vehicle more than once a year. This did wonders to feed my urge to have one relationship after another. The endless causality loop of drugs and alcohol made my life speed by rapidly. It was five years after my brother's death when tragedy struck again. Another of my brothers was killed.

He was knocked off of his tractor and crushed under it. I was in the second year of running a struggling machine shop business that I had started. One of the best qualities of my business was that my mother was the office manager. She was loving and kind and always had friendly words for everyone. I was working in the shop and she was in the office when we got the call about my brother. My vehicle was in an auto body shop, being repaired after it had hit a deer, so a coworker drove my mother and me to the accident scene.

My brother was still under the tractor when we arrived. A few other people were at the scene, but no EMS or rescue personnel. Someone yelled to us, "Do not let your mother come up here!" It was an ominous sign for sure. I ran up to the tractor as fast as I could. It was a horrible sight. My brother's twisted body was pinned to the ground in a hopeless position. His leg had a huge gash in it, but there was hardly any blood. I do not believe I had the wherewithal at that moment to realize he was most likely dead. With a wound that large, there should have been blood everywhere. I suspect his heart stopped soon after he fell under the tractor.

He had been driving the tractor across a relatively flat field, and he was not towing a wagon or any equipment. This catastrophe seemed impossible. I am not sure anybody ever came up with a reasonable explanation. The rim and hub had separated, causing the tractor to fall, but it never tipped over, and there was no reason for my brother to be underneath it. He was simply driving through the hayfield, seeing if it was ready to be cut. When I placed my hand on him, he was cold. In the distance, my mother was doubled over, with tears streaming from her eyes.

My family had spent most of the five previous years healing from my other brother's death. We had finally reached the point where we could talk about our good memories of him. He was only twenty-one years old when he died. Now, five years later, my second brother had passed away at thirty-one. My response to God this time was full-on hatred and disgust for allowing this to happen again. I felt like I could have blown up a few churches if I had any dynamite.

Following the ambulance to the hospital was a heart-wrenching experience. When the lights stopped flashing, the siren went silent, and the ambulance began traveling at the posted speed, I knew my brother was dead. I cursed God and declared my hatred toward Him. How dare He do this to my family again. I am sure I uttered many explicits that day toward the Creator of the universe. The ignorance of the words I was babbling were overshadowed only by the grief I was feeling and the severe hurt from what my parents were going through again.

He was my oldest brother and had followed in the footsteps of my father as a farmer. We really did not get along much growing up. Of course, I was the most disruptive of all the children. My oldest brother and I probably ran a close neck-and-neck race with the frustration levels that we caused our parents during our teenage years.

But something amazing happened the final year of my brother's life: We became friends. In fact, my little business sponsored a softball team that we played on together, so we spent much more time with one another than we ever did in previous years. He also cut wood for me that I burned in my shop and was a hard-working, good-hearted man. With long hair and a beard, he looked like a biker, and he even liked working on old Harleys. But to judge him by his appearance was a mistake. A gentle teddy bear is a more accurate description of who he was.

I felt cheated and shortchanged by God. We were just beginning to develop a meaningful relationship with each other, and *poof,* he was gone. I must admit, the relationship was based on worldly habits, and I am not sure if God ever came up in our conversations. At the time, it did not even dawn on me that there was more to life than self-indulgence. Sure, I would help people with this project or that project. I would enlist the help of my mechanic buddies to do repair jobs on my parents' farm. Of course, we would be thoroughly wasted by one substance or another by the end of the project. Occasionally, my brothers and I would do projects as well. We hardly partied together. A drink here or there was about it. I always felt like I needed to be in charge, as if I needed to prove something. Possibly my lack of a college degree and thoughts of not measuring up were driving factors. The effect of my second brother dying was harder than I anticipated. At that point in my life stepping into a church or having a relationship with God seemed off the table. *Romans 3:18 NKJV: "There is no fear of God before their eyes."*

I figured God was pretty much out of my life, and I would not have to bother with Him anymore. I had no respect or fear for the Creator of the universe. I was creating my own Garden of Eden. Work weeks of eighty to one hundred hours were common, and my drive to succeed was marginally stronger than my need to drink and do drugs. For many years, I was able to mix these activities with a slight edge given to success.

I met my second wife while she was working in furniture sales at a department store. In fact, the day I met her I told a friend, "That girl is going to be my wife." She was attractive and young, only nineteen years old. I was twenty-six at the time, and she was just old enough that our age difference seemed insignificant. Thinking back, I was graduating high school when she was just eleven—now that sounds creepy. She was raised in a home where regular church attendance was a part of life. In a short period of time, I was beginning to corrupt her. I convinced her to do things she thought she would never do. I am by no means boasting or proud of my despicable behavior. Someday I will be before the throne of God, and I will be giving a full account of my actions. *2 Corinthians 5:10 NKJV: "For we must all appear before the judgment seat of Christ, that each one may receive the things done in the body, according to what he has done, whether good or bad."* The day of reckoning will come, and I cannot stop it.

At the time, my divorce was not finalized from my first wife. I am sure that I deceived my new girlfriend by telling her it was already over. I would parade her around my first wife like she was the new prize I had just won. I was truly an insensitive jerk. I did not care about the thoughts and feelings of others. Once the divorce was final, my first wife felt she had the freedom to pursue another love interest. Her incredible amount of patience, prayers, suffering and hoping beyond hope were left unfulfilled because of my selfishness. Not only that, left in the wake of our divorce was a small boy who would have to suffer the consequences.

Do not ever think that your children will be okay when their parents get divorced. The inability to work out your problems should never be transferred to innocent children. We live in such a self-centered society that when the least amount of difficulty arises, we just give up. The ramifications for developing children are much more far-reaching than you can imagine. Any decency you think you have as a human being should outweigh the selfish motive to pursue what you want while leaving your children in the wake. I deeply regret that I did not understand this before it was too late. There will be a great cost for those who cause emotional, physical or psychological harm to children. *Luke 17:2 NKJV: "It would be better for him if a millstone was hung around his neck, and he were thrown into the sea, then that he should offend one of these little ones."*

Although I convinced my new girlfriend to do many things that she probably would not have done, she never participated in drug use, but she would consume alcohol with me, and we would reach a level of intoxication. Even though I was pretty upset with God and was not attending church, thoughts were stirring in me. I can remember having these drug- and alcohol-induced philosophical conversations. Somehow, I had thoughts of grandeur that I would be used by a supernatural force and even have powers of my own. Many times, I felt as though personalities from another dimension were tempting me.

I would compare these temptations almost to a contract to sell my soul. Powers of telepathy and telekinesis and the ability to actually fly through the air would be granted to me. Dreams and waking visions often floated through my awareness. *1 Peter 5:8 NKJV: "Be sober, be vigilant; because your adversary the devil walks about like a roaring lion, seeking whom he may devour."* These topics came up in conversation with my new girlfriend. I do believe it freaked her out a bit. One time, I can remember, she wrote a message on her shoe in case something happened. In tears from the heightened emotional instability caused by drugs and alcohol, I would tell her that someday I might just disappear. Little did I know that these hints of the future largely would become true, but in a supernatural and God-honoring way that I never imagined.

Of course, my understanding of these thoughts and the extreme arrogant selfishness of my behavior were totally off track. After four years of dating, my girlfriend gave me an ultimatum: "Either we get married, or I am moving on." There was a break during the four years when I tried one more time to have a successful marriage with my first wife. I had told my girlfriend that I was already divorced, which was a lie and a selfish way of convincing her to have a romantic relationship with me. She was innocent and naïve in many ways. Unfortunately, I took some of that innocence, which was not my right to do.

Fortunately for her and me, we did eventually marry. Though there seemed to be insurmountable differences between my first wife and me, I never had the spiritual clarity on the importance and reasons behind one man and one woman for life. Many years later, when my understanding began to change, this issue came up in a very powerful way. *Luke 16:18 NKJV: "Whoever divorces his wife and marries another commits adultery; and whoever marries her who is di-*

vorced from her husband commits adultery." It was so powerful that I thought I may have to divorce my second wife. That is a story unto itself that I will explain later. These last few pages may seem to be filled with boring details, but some degree of understanding is necessary.

Now that my divorce was final, and marriage was on the table for the second time, my girlfriend insisted that we be married in a church. This, of course, meant that we had to start attending one, at least in the eyes of my wife-to-be. My parents, formerly Lutherans, had switched to a Methodist church because the fiasco of my first brother's burial was too much to overcome. My girlfriend and I decided to attend the local Methodist church. The congregation included about fifty people. In 1989, three months after we started attending the church, we were married. A year or so after that, we became Sunday school teachers. My new wife taught one of the children's groups, and I taught an adult class. I definitely did not have a relationship with Jesus Christ, and I was sure I was hell bound.

My life continued as it had: working hard, drinking and doing drugs. Smoking pot was nearly as common for me as drinking water. I had convinced my new wife that it was not a big deal. I would say, "Look at how many hours I work. I deserve it." She always frowned upon it, but I managed to convince her it was not a problem. Little did I know that many of these activities opened doorways for Satanic influence in my life. *Revelation 18:23 NKJV: "The light of a lamp shall not shine in you anymore, and the voice of the bridegroom and bride shall not be heard in you anymore. For your merchants were the great men of the earth, for by your sorcery all the na-*

tions were deceived." Had someone told me that at the time, I would have said they were crazy. The depth of my foolish behavior went as far as smoking pot before the start of Sunday school class. Looking back now on those stupid decisions, I can hardly believe what I used to do. It is just an example of how deceived we can become by the tactics of Satan. One of the names for Satan is Apollyon, which means "destroyer." That is his main purpose, to destroy us, and he will do whatever is possible to achieve it.

CHAPTER 2

———

THE PATTERN THAT I HAD ESTABLISHED FOR MY lifestyle continued. In the early 1990s, some significant events took place. I am not exactly sure how or why, but God was calling me closer. My ex-wife arranged for our son to attend a Christian summer camp in Oklahoma. Even though I was going to church and teaching adult Sunday school, I was not into the God thing yet. Unfortunately, this is the position that most Christians—or so-called Christians—find themselves in. They may spend an hour or two at church, but then they live their lives however they see fit. I was guilty of this behavior for decades and now can detect it in others very easily.

I did not know much about this Christian camp, but my second wife and I decided to take my son and stay nearby while he attended it. At this point, I had become a pilot, and we had our own airplane, so we loaded up what we needed and headed out. I even took a bag of marijuana with me, because smoking pot had become a daily habit. I would never smoke in the presence of my son, but as you may know, the smell cannot be hidden. It was rare for me to take off five or six days in a row from work, because I thought so highly of my skills and therefore reasoned the business could not possibly get along without me for very long. However, the safety of my son trumped everything else.

I contacted the camp and asked if there was anything I could do to help while he was there. The person I spoke with put me in contact with the building supervisor, Roger, and he determined that I could help with some of the ongoing projects. This was great news, because I now could be on site while my nine-year-old son was there, and I could keep an eye on things. At the time, I was concerned about the possibility of crazy cult behavior or pedophile stuff going on. Unfortunately, I was not cognizant that false doctrine could be taught without my being aware of it. Knowing the Scriptures and having the ability to discern false teachers are very important. *Matthew 7:15–20 NKJV: "Beware of false prophets, who come to you in sheep's clothing, but inwardly they are ravenous wolves. You will know them by their fruits. Do men gather grapes from thorn bushes or figs from thistles? Even so, every good tree bears good fruit, but a bad tree bears bad fruit. A good tree cannot bear bad fruit, nor can a bad tree bear good fruit. Every tree that does not bear good fruit is cut down and thrown into the fire. Therefore by their fruits you will know them."*

As I look back on the mistakes I committed, I realize there is an owner's manual for life I could have used to forewarn me of the many pitfalls. If you have not realized it yet, most of the Scripture references I have made are condemnations of myself for not living the way I should have by following the Bible.

Those of you who have heard about the mysterious ways that God works will understand when I say that the ignition point of my spirit was about to take place. The first day we arrived at the camp, we checked my son in for the week's activities. The camp was set up like an Old West town, with many different building fronts: the general store, a bank, a jail and various others. There was a church service for all the kids and parents after check-in. It was a bit shocking for us to say the least. I had never been exposed to an entire congregation speaking in tongues, with seemingly no order whatsoever. We were sitting in the back, hoping to go unnoticed, but that did not happen.

As my wife and I looked at each other almost in disbelief, someone approached us. I do not remember the exact Bible scripture that they pointed out, but they were insistent that if we were saved, we also could speak in tongues. Needless to say, for me, a self-righteous, strong-willed individual, this was not the way to be introduced to speaking in tongues. My skepticism about this organization had significantly increased. I could only imagine my nine-year-old son going back to Michigan and babbling some language that no one understood. At that time, I had no understanding of speaking in tongues. I was convinced that these people were a bunch of wackos.

My wife and I reluctantly allowed my son to spend the first night at the camp, and we returned to our nearby hotel room, where I soon partook in my daily ritual of smoking pot. We discovered that first night at the hotel that we were very close to railroad tracks. About 3 a.m. every morning, we were awoken by the hotel windows shaking and the startling sound of a train whizzing by. The first morning, after breakfast, we headed back to the camp to meet with Roger, the building supervisor.

He was a middle-aged fellow with a gravelly voice, and he seemed to have lived a rough life. He had numerous tattoos, which were not in vogue with the general public at that time. In the '90s, tattoos were associated with motorcycle gangs. Sure enough, he had been a Hell's Angels member at one time and had been shot and stabbed several times during his days as a motorcycle outlaw. His numerous scars were obviously caused by deep gashes. As I peer back into time with the lenses of Jesus Christ adjusting my vision, I can see Roger for what he really was.

His manner of speech was methodical and measured, with great care given to the value and placement of each word, but his vocabulary was no frills and simple. When he conveyed an important message to me, his eyes locked on to mine as if my life depended on listening to him. Roger told me that the reason I was there had nothing to do with my son going to camp. "God told me you are here to receive the Holy Spirit," he said.

"Here we go," I thought, "a bunch of wackos talking in tongues or whatever it was the night before, and now this guy standing beside me is telling me that God is talking to him about me."

I just about had enough of this garbage and was ready to walk away. Roger put his hand on my shoulder and said, "Come with me. We need to go down by the river, so I can pray for you."

My mind was screaming, "Get out of here as quick as you can!" But when Roger laid his hand on me, I felt nearly paralyzed. I could not begin to conceive what was happening. When Roger started walking away it was as if a string were tied around his waist and connected to mine. He would take a step, and I would take a step. This continued all the way to the river. The distance between us never altered more than a few inches. I felt as though I was in a waking dream state. Nobody else was around, just the two of us. At least that is what I thought, but there was somebody else there. *Matthew 18:20 NKJV: "For where two or three are gathered together in my name, I am there in the midst of them."*

Most of my adult life, I was known to be a pretty tough guy. I am not sure if I even cried when my first brother died, but I think I shed a few tears for my second brother. What happened when Roger started praying for me was totally out of character for me. As the earnest words flowed from Roger, my tears pounded down like Niagara Falls. He prayed that I would receive the Holy Spirit, while I didn't even know what that meant. But judging from my physical response, something was happening. When he finished praying, he affirmed, "Your life is going to change."

We returned to the camp buildings and began constructing porch railings. I felt different, like my understanding was somehow transformed, but I really did not understand how or why. That evening, I returned to my wife at the motel. She had helped in another area of the camp that day, so she was oblivious to what had transpired with me. I told her the story, and she was probably more skeptical than I was. With both hands on her hips she stated, "I have been going to a Baptist church my whole life, but I have never heard of this Holy Spirit stuff."

Our dispute lasted several days. I told her that all I knew was that something was different. Our disagreements spilled into the weekend, and I left her behind when I went to church on Sunday. We were still in Oklahoma, and she did not have to walk far to get to the church, but that was no excuse, because it was still a power play for me to exercise my dominance over her. Even though I felt something called the Holy Spirit, I did not immediately change. The reality is that even now, I am still in the process of changing.

My daily pot smoking continued, but my enjoyment of it was diminishing. Several times in the past I had tried to kick the habit, but I never achieved more than a few weeks of sobriety before I was drawn back into the hideous habit.

A couple weeks after my return from Oklahoma, I was out jogging by myself on a gravel country road when I heard a voice say, "Cast out Natavia!" I looked around, and all that was staring back at me was row after row of corn stalks. After scanning the area in all directions, I realized wherever the voice, sensation or waking dream was coming from was not visible.

I distinctly remember thinking, "This is great, now I am hearing voices." I am sure my thoughts were as sarcastic as they could be. A few seconds passed before I heard the voice again: "If you want to stop smoking pot, cast out Natavia." I knew nothing about spiritual warfare, demonic oppression, demonic possession, or gateway activities that open us to all types of evil influence and negative energy. I thought, "What do I have to lose?" So I said out loud, "I cast away the Natavia." Jesus likely chuckled or shook his head at my ignorance. Once again, I needed further instruction: "If you want to stop smoking pot, cast away Natavia in the name of Jesus."

This time, I said it exactly the way I was supposed to. At

that moment, I felt something being removed from my body. *Matthew 12:28 NKJV: "But if I cast out demons by the spirit of God surely the kingdom of God has come upon you."* The experience was unique and exhilarating. I felt lighter, faster, clearer in my thoughts. The pace of my run the rest of the way home seemed twice as fast as normal, but my exertion level seemed lower, which was amazing.

At the time I was living in an apartment upstairs from my shop. When I returned to the apartment from my run, I located my rolling tray, papers and weed and declared to my wife that I was done smoking pot. She looked at me with an expression that implied a groan and said, "Sure, whatever you say." Many times she had heard such proclamations. She knew that most likely it was just another vain attempt. I told her about the Natavia thing. I do not believe that gave her any comfort. If anything, it gave her major concern.

Now that marijuana is becoming legal in more and more states, I am sure there will be many who disagree with my assumptions about it. I believed that my thinking was deeper, more insightful, and enhanced overall by marijuana. I was totally wrong, and it was only when I was set free from the addiction that I understood. My abilities to engineer, design and invent increased dramatically. Things that I would have stumbled around and taken weeks to figure out now were only a couple quick thoughts away. For years after I quit smoking pot, the ideas flowed from me like water from an open water faucet. Unfortunately, I used the abilities that God had given me to become more and more arrogant. Something much greater happened than some spirit being removed from me.

I had the sensation God had given me a special blessing that restored my mind and replaced all of the brain cells that I had destroyed through drug and alcohol abuse. Not only that, God rearranged some of the neural pathways to work far more efficiently. This is a bit speculative, but I have no other way to explain the drastic change that seemed to happen overnight. Through this transformation, God was giving me the opportunity for significant success in my life. I believe it was a covenant contract that God made with me: "Stay away from the pot and follow me, and I will make you fishers of men." The problem was that God kept his word better than I did.

This is the trigger point that led to the start of my journey to *How to Piss Off God*. Yet twenty-plus years would pass before I reached the end. Through the power of God I was able to stop smoking pot, but I struggled in many other areas. My selfishness and arrogance dominated my life. Not long after these events, God showed me a few things.

One night, I experienced a vision that to this day is still vivid, though it happened more than two decades ago. I walked into a grand hall, like a room in Buckingham Palace. There was an ornate wooden desk with elaborately carved adornments. The ceiling was about twenty feet tall. The room felt exquisite but cold, what you would expect to find in a palace. I was standing in front of the desk when another person entered the room. He was a handsome man who appeared to be a flawless specimen in his prime. His medium skin tone complemented his white suit. His appearance was pleasant, and his smile was welcoming as he motioned for me to sit down in front of the desk. Initially our conversation was light.

Something inside me was warning me to be cautious. I had the feeling that the handsome individual in front of me was something different. "Who are you?" I asked. A stack of papers sat on the desk, in front of him. He looked down at the papers, and a glowing ribbon began to consume them. When the papers were gone, nothing remained, no ashes, just the clean top of the desk. I looked at the man and asked, "Are you Satan?"

With a smug look he responded, "So what if I am?"

I volleyed back, "You are going to be sent to hell."

He chuckled at my boldness.

For whatever reason, I had a Stanley tape measure connected to my belt. I placed it in front of me on the desk. Satan slammed his hands down and demanded, "Who are you?" I looked down at the Stanley tape measure, which had begun to spin slowly. One rotation, two rotations, three rotations.

He stood up and leaned halfway over the desk, his eyes piercing right through me, and stated, "You are the transfigurer."

I replied, "I do not know what you are talking about. I am just a man, nothing special." Then I told him again, "You are going to hell."

He sat back down in his chair with a smirk on his face. "Then," he said, pointing over my left shoulder, "you think those two are going to send me to hell?"

I turned and looked, and there were God and Jesus, standing side by side. They looked ordinary, but the peace and love that emanated from them was undeniable. I could have closed my eyes and still sensed their presence. I returned my gaze to Satan, who was now standing up. He walked around the desk toward me and said, "Transfigurer, ha," like I was his next opponent in an MMA ring.

He came around my side of the desk. My chair instantly swung 90 degrees toward him. I felt paralyzed. His presence sunk deep inside me. Absolute horror and terror consumed me. I looked over at Jesus and cried out, "Jesus, save me please! Jesus, save me!"

Satan continued to get comfortable in my body, occupying more and more space inside me. Now, he was nearly completely in my body, and his head was leaning back into my head. The last bit of me that was left called, "Jesus, save me! Please save me!" At the very last instant, when I thought there was no hope left, something happened. My body shuddered, and I sobbed, realizing this was prophecy.

Little did I know this was exactly what was going to happen over the next twenty-plus years. For the first time ever, I had the feeling that something in my life would be measuring the time that Satan had left. Maybe as the story continues to unfold, there will be more answers. I only wish I had the wisdom at the time to understand how monumental of a warning I was given. God gave me a vision of what would happen in my life if I did not focus on Jesus. In fact, a few weeks later, he gave me the opportunity to participate in His will. That opportunity should have been enough to keep me on the path of righteousness. Had I proclaimed the glory of how God's light shines into this world, things would have been different. Instead, I hid the story from just about everybody for many years—a big mistake. *Matthew 5:14-16 NKJV: "You are the light of the world. A light that is set on a hill cannot be hidden. Nor do they light a lamp and put it under a basket, but on a lampstand, and it gives light to all who are in the house. Let your light so shine before men, that they may see your good works and glorify your father in heaven."*

My wife and I were in a service at our local church, when, about halfway through the message, the idea was planted in my mind. I was a Sunday school teacher for an adult class at that time, and my wife led a junior high school class. Ironically, my class included the parents of a girl who was in my wife's class. A few months earlier, the young girl began to experience severe health issues. She ended up at the University of Michigan CS Mott Children's Hospital. The doctors there discovered a brain tumor that was inoperable, so the young girl was sent home and hospice was called in. Her weight dropped from 120 pounds to 60. The parents had already chosen a burial dress and casket for the young girl. She was now in a near comatose state at home with death knocking at her door.

When God's instruction was given to me, it took my breath away, so much so that I gasped for air. The instruction was, "Go to this girl's house this very instant and pray for her." The feeling was so strong that I began to panic a bit. I felt as though I was being held in a bear hug by some supernatural force that was saying, "You will do this."

I leaned over to my wife and said, "We have to leave now." She gave me a perplexed look and said, "Just wait. He will be done talking in ten minutes." I warned, "If we do not leave now, I feel like I am going to die." We left mid-service, with many eyes turned toward us as we walked out.

We had never been to the girl's house before, so I believe

we looked in a phone book to find the address. When we arrived, we knocked on the door. My wife still did not understand what was going on. I explained to the parents the best I could that I was here to pray for their daughter. Somewhat reluctantly, they ushered me into the room where she was lying on a bed. She was skin and bones, with sunken cheeks, a shadow of her former self. As the father exited the room, I took her fragile hand in mine, saying, "I really do not even know why I am here, and I am not sure what I am supposed to say. What I do know beyond a shadow of doubt is that Jesus wanted me to pray for you. I am just going to pray that somehow you pull through this and are healed. In Jesus' name, amen."

That was it, short and to the point. While I was praying, the mother showed my wife the dress they had picked out for the girl's burial. We said our goodbyes and departed their house. Throughout the remainder of the day, my wife and I talked about what happened. Neither of us grasped the magnitude of the situation. I did feel as though the miraculous deliverance from pot addiction and the prayer to receive the Holy Spirit were beginning to affect my life. I was such a baby in my understanding of things, because not much of it made any sense or was absorbed. A week or so later, we heard an update on the girl's condition.

She had regained consciousness and some cognitive ability, so she was taken back to the hospital. Doctors did a brain scan and discovered that a cellular water pocket had formed around the tumor and expanded, pushing the brain away from it. I am sure I am not using the proper terms, but this is the best way for me to explain it. What was once inoperable, now was operable. The doctors were able to go in and remove the tumor, and the young girl, now a woman, is alive today. Was this some fluke of the nature? Was it supernatural intervention? One thing for sure is that it was not caused by me. I was just an observer of God's power. Nothing in this world will ever convince me of anything different.

This is the point where I should have been singing praises to the glory of God. I should have been telling everyone how miraculously God worked. You would think that an arrogant, self-centered person like me would have touted what I had done as a badge of honor. Instead, I didn't mention it for decades, not even to my son.

As I reflect on this experience, I realize now it may have been one of the most important events in my life, and one of the biggest opportunities to operate under God's will instead of my own. I think my wife was part of this experience so that she could be the witness who confirms that it happened as stated. If such an event were to occur today, our understanding of it would be vastly different from what it was then. God was giving me a preview of what He wanted my life to be, or I could let the things of this world (Satan) absorb me until there was nothing left.

CHAPTER 3

———

THE RECENT EVENTS IN MY LIFE HAD LEFT ME feeling spiritually unfulfilled and that I needed to find a better teacher. We ended up searching for another church and found First Church of God, Lansing Avenue. At the first service we attended, we felt like we had found our new home. We quickly became friends with the pastor and his family, and we would even babysit their children. Pastor Rick was a wonderful man with a heart to serve God. He was multitalented, with piano-playing and singing abilities that matched his oratory skills. He and his family were a lot of fun to spend time with. I never thought that I would have a pastor as a friend. I think that was largely because I had lived such a sinful life.

Through the efforts of Pastor Rick, my wife and I grew in our understanding. For a couple of years, I cleaned up my act. I did not drink or use drugs, and I was even reading the Bible on a regular basis. Every Wednesday morning at 7 o'clock, Rick would meet with my wife and me. We had these little brown discipleship books, and during the week, we would read our Bibles and fill in answers to the questions in our books. When we met with Rick, we reviewed our answers and enjoyed fellowship with each other. We enjoyed numerous hearty laughs together; I had never thought that hanging around a pastor could be so much fun. My business was doing fairly well, but when I made some steps toward God, it began to grow extremely fast. I always thought that this was God's blessing, but I am not so sure now. Satan is in charge of this world and all the temptations that are in it.

On Friday afternoons, we would shut down the shop and travel around the neighborhood. We would go to people's houses randomly and talk to them about life, God and community. The fruits of these efforts sometimes took years to materialize. Most people were receptive and courteous to us. My wife and I would go together, sometimes with coworkers. I can remember baptizing a guy in a swimming pool behind the shop. While I was talking to him about God, I asked him why he should be let into heaven. He looked right at me and said, "I got me a dog and I treat him pretty good." That was the only time in my life I heard a response like that. After I explained to him what the Bible instructs, we prayed together. He then asked if we could baptize him. Those were wonderful times, and I felt like I was participating in something much bigger than myself.

Eventually Pastor Rick and his family moved to a different church. We pretty much lost contact with each other. My wife and I took the proceeds from our business and built a new house. We never had a mortgage payment. I felt as though it was God's blessing that provided the money to build the house, so before we moved in, we elevated an eighteen-foot-tall steel cross on our front lawn. Believe it or not, that caused some commotion in my family.

Apparently, my brother, who lived next door, had over-heard someone talking at the gas station about a Ku Klux Klan cross that had been erected in front of a house. My brother spoke to my parents about it, and they told me they thought I should take it down. I couldn't see anything wrong with the cross, so I asked God for guidance. "If you want this cross taken down," I prayed, "you have to hit me over the head with a two-by-four." Initially, the cross was painted white, and I changed the color to a light tan. The odd thing is, my parents and my brother had attended church their entire lives. I have to believe it was Satan's tactics to cause a commotion over something he did not like. Most people are completely oblivious to the reality of the unseen world. I put myself in that category for many, many years.

As my business continued to succeed and enhanced my ability to live in an even more wasteful, self-centered fash-ion, my life did not improve. All the things I acquired gave me only short-lived satisfaction. I do not want to give the impression that we never did anything to help others, how-ever, many times we did things out of a sense of guilt. The sole purpose was to somehow justify the extravagant spend-ing that I did for many years. There were times when my good acts were heartfelt and done in secrecy, but there were also times when I would purposely draw attention to myself. God does not accept that behavior. *Matthew 6:1–4 NKJV: "Take heed that you do not do your charitable deeds before men, to be seen by them. Otherwise you have no reward from your father in heaven. Therefore, when you do a charitable deed, do not sound a trumpet before you as the hypocrites do in the syna-gogues and in the streets, that they may have glory from men.*

Assuredly, I say to you, they have their reward. But when you do a charitable deed, do not let your left hand know what your right hand is doing, that your charitable deed may be in secret; and your father who sees in secret will himself reward you openly."

Little by little, the cares of the world pulled me back into their malevolence. My focus on God was diminishing as was my time reading His Word.

By the late-1990s, my mental well-being was practically nonexistent. The workload that I forced upon myself was nearly unbearable. I had a debt-free business and a new house that we built while I was hovering on the edge of a nervous breakdown. I would come home many nights in tears because mentally I was totally spent. Working seven days a week for many years was finally taking its toll. I would get up early Sunday morning to go and work for three or four hours. Then I would go home, get cleaned up, and go to church. Usually within an hour after I returned home, I would go back to work. That was my break for the week. *Mark 8:36 NKJV: "For what will it profit a man if he gains the whole world, and loses his own soul?"*

I once worked sixty-nine out of seventy-two hours and felt practically psychotic while doing it. I prayed that Jesus would take me, because I did not want to live another day. The business had become my captor, and there was no way to escape. I was a micromanager fully convinced that no one could do the job as well as I could. God had given me the clarity of thought that made most situations very easy, however, I exercised zero humility in how I directed that power. Most engineering and invention tasks that I undertook were like reading the words off a piece of paper. I needed hardly any effort to understand what I was seeing. Had I not been so full of myself and instead concentrated my efforts on being a good teacher, my tasks would have been far more manageable.

Please do not misunderstand my explanation as a plea for sympathy. I brought on most of the problems I experienced. I cannot imagine how carefree my life would have been if I had been focused on Christ. Many times in my life, God reminded me that financial success had nothing to do with eternal joy, but I was too selfish to see the many warnings that He put before me.

My mother worked as our office manager for the first twelve years of the business. She and my father were concerned that I would not be able to bear the intense pressure much longer. In 1999, by which point the business had become quite profitable, I was approached by a gentleman interested in buying it. This was the first offer I had received, and I accepted it.

I was a country boy who still believed a man's word was to be honored at all costs. My attorney warned me against the deal. Being at the end of my rope psychologically probably blinded my sense of reason. My lack of judgment ended up costing us dearly. Within three years, the business had lost every one of its customers. The bank took over all the assets, and I had to go to an auction and buy back things I was never paid for.

Something miraculous happened during this time. Again, God was blessing us even though I did not deserve it. For nearly ten years, my wife and I had been trying to have a child. We tried many different procedures, but all without luck. Finally, doctors discovered that she had endometriosis. She had surgery to remove one her ovaries completely and half of the other, so we were fearful that we would never get pregnant. Because I had sold the business, we were able to take our first one-week vacation ever; we visited Maui. While there, we went to a small church with a couple dozen Hawaiians. The pastor asked if we had any prayer requests, so I raised my hand and shared, "We have been trying to get pregnant for ten years." My wife gave me a disgusted look, as if to say, "What are you doing?"

At that point, everyone in the church gathered around us. They laid their hands on us and prayed. We did not think a lot about it at the time, however, we had quite a shock five weeks after we returned home. My wife had a scheduled appointment with the fertility doctor. She had been monitoring her temperature, and right away, the nurse was curious about her chart. During an ultrasound, a heartbeat was detected. The doctor informed my wife that she was about six weeks pregnant. After ten years, and the loss of one and a half ovaries, this was miraculous to us. If you are not convinced that this was a miracle, you will be when you hear of the return trip we made to the hospital when our daughter was twelve.

This was a very enjoyable time in our lives. The responsibilities I had were significantly decreased, and I was able to enjoy the first few years of my daughter's life before returning to a chaotic work schedule.

I had started a small machine-building business after selling my manufacturing company. There were only two of us running the business, and we stayed busy and did well. As you may have guessed, I am not the type of person who can just sit around doing nothing. Once again, God was blessing my efforts. The money that we made ended up being used to get my former business back into shape.

I initially used most of the money I earned to pay taxes and fund self-promoting endeavors. The situation that I found myself in was dismal. Not only did I have to buy things back, I had to pay back taxes on the building in order to keep it. This was an extremely troubling time in our lives. I had dedicated fifteen years to starting and growing a business, and now most of that effort netted far less than we anticipated.

On top of that, I spent a lot of money supposedly promoting a program that showcased workers who use their hands. But in doing so, I wasted most of the money promoting myself. We had a chopper built by some famous motorcycle builders who had a television show. This eventually allowed me to be on the TV show. I met the production crew and through that introduction became the main character in a few episodes of a new show. God already knew my ego was too big. I am so glad he did not allow me to have any success in television. Any kind of fame would have been disastrous for me.

I also sponsored a NASCAR car for one race. My stupidity had me under the illusion that if I spent enough money, it would grant me greater success. However, something good did come from these experiences. The hands-on program turned out to be a worthy cause for kids. But because of my poor business decisions and self-promoting, life became tough once again. What we assumed was an early retirement fund became something far different.

The financial hole we found ourselves in forced us to borrow money for food. The situation was reminiscent of when I started the business. Back then, for more than ten years, I lived in the shop and burned wood because we could not afford a furnace. We did not have a refrigerator, so we kept our food outside in the winter and in a cooler during the summer. We could not afford to wine and dine our customers, so we grew a patch of sweetcorn behind the shop. Every year, we would fill crates with sweetcorn and send it to our main customers. Slowly, I made the apartment upstairs livable, and eventually we got a furnace and refrigerator. Even with such humble beginnings, I still had a cocky and arrogant attitude.

Now, we were living in a nice home that was fully equipped. Even my parents, who had never sued anybody in their lives, suggested I take the businessman who had ruined by company to court. I distinctly remember that God pressed me not to sue anyone, but to simply work hard and trust that everything would be okay. Fortunately, I had not burned any bridges with my customers. Most of them were ecstatic that I was going back into business. It was 2003 when I got the business back and restarted the work schedule that had nearly killed me. The first few years, I built machines for customers.

A guy I knew had taken on some of the work from my main customer. He was renting space down the road, and he later needed additional space, so he moved into the building I occupied. We would end up buying him out and expanding into other areas. Once again, the sounds of mechanical machinery producing parts were heard throughout the building.

A couple of the guys who had worked for that former main customer of mine approached me about going into business with them. I was hesitant, but my greed and need to succeed once again overpowered my concerns. There were just two of us initially; the other guy joined us later.

Several dishonest and illegal actions occurred. Company secrets and tooling designs were taken and used to compete against the company they had worked for. Also, equipment and tooling would show up with no invoice. I turned my head many times to these wrongdoings, which means I was just as guilty as they were. *Proverbs 10:2 NKJV: "Treasures of wickedness profit nothing, but righteousness delivers from death."* One day, I went into the conference room and saw tooling blueprints from my partners' former company being copied. I told one partner that this was unacceptable and would have to stop. I later discovered similar things continued to happen behind my back. These guys felt their former company owed them something even though they had been well compensated for their services. One of the guys who was supposed to become a partner but never did said they had a storage area filled with all the tooling blueprints.

By now, my son had graduated from college and was married to his high school sweetheart. Many times he had worked at the company during the summer. Now he was working as a production supervisor, and some of his bad decisions led to disagreements between him and one of the partners. As the disagreements continued, it became clear that my partners' dishonest behavior and selective memory were still a mode of operation.

A silent partner behind the scenes was manipulating

much of the situation. I never really trusted the man because of the many dishonest things he had done in his career. Some of them cost me several hundred thousand dollars. But after many years, I came to trust him. I thought maybe we had become friends, but it was clear by his actions that he always had an ulterior motive.

One partner was on the scene, and I decided it would be best that we went our separate directions when our business practices and growth strategies began to differ. Plus, I had been captain of my own ship for nearly twenty years, which made it very difficult to share control with partners, especially ones who early on put forth no effort. The fact that I felt my son was being treated unfairly, even though he had contributed somewhat to the situation, made the decision even easier.

In 2007, we dissolved the partnership, but our businesses continued to interact with each other. My son became the plant manager of the new facility and helped us achieve our first quality certification. Unfortunately, I was still arrogant, overbearing and a tough fighter. The problem for me was that my son was very strong willed himself, yet I do not believe the negative characteristics that I possessed had manifested nearly as much in him. He was willing to stand up to me, and I made it quite a struggle for him to exist in that environment. He chose to work smarter, not longer. I would always judge others by the standard that I set, but this standard was totally unreasonable, unsustainable and unnecessary. At the time, however, there was no way I could be convinced of that. Eventually, my controlling manipulation drove him away. The freedom from the business that I was hoping to attain vanished when he and his wife moved to Nashville.

Pretty much this entire time, I was pursuing things of the world. I had not read the Bible for years, and I would drink alcohol much more than I should. There was a three-week period when I drank a half-pint of Captain Morgan's every day, working sixteen or eighteen hours a day. The amount of alcohol that I consumed was just enough to take the edge off and make my life bearable. Had I been seeking God for my strength, and spending time in the Word and in prayer, the drinking would have been unnecessary. You see, when we become fixated on our life and things of this world, we become useless to the Kingdom. There is no spiritual warfare because you are already serving Satan, whether you realize it or not. Please understand, if your life mimics any part of what I have experienced, you are trying to serve two masters, which means you are serving Satan.

God is not looking for pinch hitters or bench sitters. Your life must be fully surrendered and totally occupied with playing on the team. Your thoughts, actions and behaviors should revolve around serving Jesus Christ. *James 4:7 NKJV: "Therefore submit to God, resist the devil, and he will flee from you."* The many years that I was lukewarm to God are heartbreaking now and were a terrible waste of my life. I do not want to go more than a few pages without continually reminding you of that. Please, never consider that this behavior is somehow okay or acceptable.

I always loved my son very much, and it was difficult when he and his wife moved to Nashville. The first few months, we really did not talk much. I think he was far angrier with me than I realized. He was smart enough to understand that giving up your entire life for success was not worth it. Some key statements that he made to me had an impact. He told me my life had boiled down to accomplishing incredible things over the weekend so that I could brag about how much I got done. He would always acknowledge the genius behind my engineering skills. Instead of giving glory to God, as I should have, I puffed myself up. God restored those abilities and enhanced them when he delivered me from my pot addiction. Unfortunately, I took all the credit for many years.

Many times, people would ask about my success. I would attribute it to growing up on a farm and watching my father repair all kinds of equipment. He did not have a nice machine shop or suitable equipment to do repairs efficiently, however, he had skills and ingenuity and somehow would figure out how to make things work again. Then I would give a list of other reasons for my great engineering abilities, which did not include God. Just so you know, I am saying this with a sarcastic tone. I would say I was successful because of which country I was born in, the state, the economic climate, the need for manufacturing, the right learning opportunities, adequate mental capacity, good health—the list went on and on.

Often, my wife would throw in God's blessing as an explanation for my success. I was almost always offended by her saying that. After all, I was the one who worked eighty-plus hours a week for decades. I was the one who would not give up. I was the one who believed failure was not an option. I was the one who would do whatever it took to succeed. Whatever else I could think of, I would use to showcase myself. *Proverbs 29:23 NKJV: "A man's pride will bring him low, but the humble in spirit will retain honor."* In such a success-driven society, we have adopted behaviors and mindsets that are totally wrong. I wish my eyes had been opened much sooner to the reality of this verse, and that I had understood it years ago. *1 Corinthians 1:31 NKJV: "That, as it is written, he who glories, let him glory in the Lord."*

CHAPTER 4

WHEN I WAS FORCED TO TAKE BACK THE BUSINESS, I felt as though God was saying, "Just work hard, and it will be okay." I questioned His wisdom—a stupid thing to do, I know. However, as with everything else in my life, He was right. What took fifteen years to accomplish before was surpassed in five years this time. The revenue was greater, the stress was a bit less, and I just continued on my path of arrogant behavior. Here is the amazing thing about God: He never gives up on us. I have come to understand that He miraculously restored my mental capacity so that I could give Him all the glory.

My desire to put the spotlight on myself continued. We had designed and built little wheelie cars for our hands-on program for kids. We came up with the crazy idea of choreographing the movements of the wheelie cars to a popular song. I traveled to Texas to audition for *America's Got Talent*. We actually made it to the standby list and thought we were going to be on national TV. At this point, it was only the second or third season, and the producers thought the wheelie cars were a bit dangerous. Again, God saved me from drawing too much attention to myself, which would have resulted in my being more of an a-hole. A for arrogant, because I was too full of myself to realize anything different.

A year or so before my son departed the business, I hired a young woman fresh out of college. She and I worked on several projects together, and she was quite talented. I piled more and more responsibilities on her as time went on. Eventually, we had an opportunity to go to Jay Leno's garage in California and take a little wheelie car with us. We had free rein to walk around his garage and assist in the installation of a wind generator that some of the kids from the shop classes had worked on. We were invited to visit the garage as part of the installation crew and to meet Jay.

Instead of viewing this as an opportunity to showcase the kids, I tried to twist it for my own glorification. *John 5:44 NKJV: "How can you believe, who receive honor from one another, and do not seek to honor that comes from the only God?"* The funny thing was, the young woman who worked with me ended up appearing briefly in an episode of Jay's TV show. We had taken many photos and videos of our interactions with Jay. However, it became so frustrating trying to deal with NBC that we never posted one picture or video. This too ended up being a huge waste of time and money. Had my motives been purer and more worthwhile, the outcome could have been much different.

Life continued, and I was still fully in the driver's seat of what I chose to do. One of the main struggles for me and those who worked with me was the constant flood of ideas. I was far more interested in making an invention that worked than marketing it. Once I had something operational, I would usually lose interest.

On a September morning in 2011, I got a call that no one ever wants to receive. My father, who was eighty-one years old, was passed out on the floor of his home, unresponsive. I left work and rushed to his house, where EMTs were trying to resuscitate him. My mother, in the next room with my sisters, was distraught. Ultimately, my father passed away that day, and my mother was left behind alone. She had dementia, which had gone undiagnosed for several years.

My father was a good-hearted, lovable individual who always had a story to tell. We considered him the PR person of our business. Often, he would do deliveries and pick up items that we needed. As painful as it was to see him move to a holy realm, it was his time. Various body functions were becoming difficult, and he knew his time was short. The last few weeks of his life, he seldom made eye contact with people. I believe it was his way of severing the connection to this world and preparing himself for the next. After he passed away, I began considering my own mortality. Now it was time to look after my mother.

For the next two years, my siblings and I made it a priority to assist in her care. She was a wonderful woman who lived a selfless life her entire time here on earth. Her actions toward others demonstrated a spiritual understanding that few possess. Had I modeled my life after hers, I would not have experience so much disappointment. She was more interested in fulfilling the desires of the spirit than the flesh. *Galatians 5:16–17 NKJV: "I say then: walk in the spirit, and you shall not fulfill the lust of the flesh. For the flesh lusts against the spirit, and the Spirit against the flesh; and these are contrary to one another, so that you do not do the things that you wish."* I very much anticipate the day when I can be in her presence again.

Over the years, my son and I became good friends once again. He continued to live in Nashville and was very successful at his job. His wife was a surgical nurse and was doing well in her profession. One morning, I was sitting in church and had this flood of ideas about wearable technology. My son was the first one I called to discuss it. Ultimately, we were able to work together again, but this time he was in charge of his own ship. We planned a trip to Las Vegas for the Consumer Electronics Show, to investigate the potential competition and what was going on in the space that my son's company was operating in. The day before we were going to head out to Las Vegas something happened.

I completed my forty-minute workout, and as was my typical routine for a Sunday morning, I was getting ready to go to work for a few hours before church. I felt a strange numbness in both elbows and a tingling sensation in my hands. I thought maybe I had overexerted myself and decided to head to work anyway. The drive to work took only about ten minutes. Halfway there, the tingling increased. I decided it would be best to return home. I am sure that God influenced that decision, because had I gone to work and lost consciousness, no one would have been there to notice. I was experiencing the onset of a heart attack. When I returned home, I called my brother, who had worked in the medical field for decades. I told him the symptoms, and he advised me to go to the emergency room right away.

As soon as we got to the hospital, the staff hooked me up to a machine and realized I was having a heart attack. Within a few minutes, I was surrounded by nurses, doctors and the hospital chaplain. Apparently, the artery that was plugged runs down the front side of the heart and is called the widow-maker. It concerned me that the hospital chaplain was questioning me about my faith. I had not realized the severity of the situation. Within twenty minutes, I was in surgery, having three stents put in my heart to open up three blocked arteries. The staff did a great job, and I was out of the hospital in only four days.

Surviving the heart attack had nothing to do with my choices or the expertise of the staff. God had orchestrated the chain of events to lead me in a direction. Many of you may think this sounds far-fetched, maybe even delusional. Regardless of what you think, there are things that are hard to explain. Why did I decide to turn around and go back home? I was a tough guy who rarely went to the doctor and worked my way through just about any situation. What if this occurred thirty hours later? I would have been 35,000 feet in the air, somewhere between Michigan and Las Vegas.

But these coincidences do not even register on the scale of what was to come. This event prompted a significant change in myself and my priorities. Before you jump to any conclusions, thinking that this was my come-to-Jesus moment, I will just tell you it was not. I simply decided it was time to stop working and enjoy life.

As unbelievable as it seemed, I just stepped away from the business. I mean completely and immediately. Remember the young gal who I hired, who went out to Jay Leno's garage with me? Whether she wanted to or not, she took over the responsibility of running the business. She was only twenty-six years old, but her team, against all odds, pulled it off. There were several dedicated employees who worked a number of years with me. They had the capability to succeed, but they always relied on me. This points to the fact that I was not a good leader and did not empower them to the level I should have. This young woman was somehow able to pull everyone together and make it all work. She became one of the region's youngest manufacturing-company presidents. Her success made me realize I was not nearly as valuable and irreplaceable as I thought. In fact, in many areas, she did a much better job than I did.

Hopefully, I have been successful in showing you how God demonstrated his love and mercy for me for many years. The reason why I am giving you so many details about the progression of my life is to show you how unworthy I am. Year after year, I denied the Lordship of Jesus and basically said, "It is okay. I got this covered." I wish I could tell you this was a turning point and that I started getting better. However, that was not the case. When my life eventually was revealed to me the way God sees it, I was heartbroken.

I could give you a whole list of good things that I did, but that would sound like justification. When you have selfish motives and a pride-filled heart, they nullify just about anything good that you do. So, if I occasionally indicate a good action that I did, disregard it. Only because of Jesus, who lives through me, can there be actions that are notable. *2 Corinthians 4:6–7 NKJV: "For it is the God who commanded the light to shine out of darkness, who has shown in our hearts to give the light of the knowledge of the glory of God in the face of Jesus Christ. But we have this treasure in earthen vessels, that the excellence of the power may be of God and not of us."*

After I went through the recovery process from the heart attack, I started working on trails at my home. We had access to a large area of woods and open fields. Months led to years, and I developed a whole network of trails. With help from others, I put up my first zip line. I think it was inspired by a return trip to Maui, where we rode on zip lines that were nearly a mile long. The top speed was over seventy miles an hour, and at points, we were six hundred feet off the ground. Being an adrenaline junkie always led me to these types of activities, but there was something far more spectacular that took place on that trip.

The year we returned to Hawaii was 2013, when our daughter was twelve years and three months old. We thought it would be interesting to visit the church where the congregation had prayed for us to have a child. I was out for a bike ride early on a Sunday morning and my wife was online, trying to find that little church. When I returned, she was frustrated. She had landed on a church's webpage and was unable to get off it. She had tried everything she could think of except for rebooting the computer. She was sure that it was not the church that we wanted, however, it turned out that it was. I guess God did not want her going to another website.

We got ready and proceeded to the little church. We drove by the street that it was on several times before we found it. Finally, realizing that the church was right before our eyes, I parked our vehicle. We recognized the gentleman who was directing cars from when we met him thirteen years ago. Based on the number of cars parked around the church, it appeared the membership had doubled or tripled.

Quickly, we exited the vehicle and went into the church. I located the pastor and told him that I had a testimony that I wanted to share. He was a different pastor from the one we had seen thirteen years earlier. My daughter acted timid and reserved. During that stage of her life, it was not normal. Even though I was not walking with the Lord, I sensed something powerful was present. We were surprised when the pastor started his sermon.

He showed several YouTube videos of people walking into plate-glass doors and then used those videos as the basis for his sermon. He said that we must always be on guard and aware. A lot of times, things that trip us up are right in front of us. *1 Corinthians 16:13–14 NKJV: "Watch, stand fast in the faith, be brave, be strong. Let all that you do be done with love."* My family and I looked at each other during the showing of the videos. Two weeks earlier, we were at a pizza parlor when our daughter walked into a plate-glass door and broke the glass. This ended up being a prophetic proclamation over our daughter. When she was sixteen years old she had a situation that occurred in plain sight, so to speak. Through the power of God's protection, she escaped certain disaster.

When the service concluded, the pastor allowed me to speak. I told the story of how we were here thirteen years earlier, and I pointed at my daughter and said, "This is the result." Many people came up and spoke with her, and she was overwhelmed. She was always tough-minded, with a commander spirit, so when she was overtaken by tears brought on by the presence of the Holy Spirit, she did not know how to react. She wanted to leave the church quickly, almost to the point of being rude. I told her when we got in the car that she was experiencing the presence of the Holy Spirit. I really did not know what I was talking about, because my experience in such matters was very limited at that point. But my assumption was correct and most likely inspired by God.

When we returned to the hotel, our daughter was totally wiped. We had never seen her like that. She slept for three or four hours. She had not taken a nap since she was an infant. When she awoke, she was very vocal about the fact that she did not enjoy the experience. I kept reassuring her that it was a great thing and she should cherish it. She didn't know it, but that was a starting point in her helping me.

This is when she began pointing out my excessive lifestyle and unnecessary purchases. Although she did not know Jesus Christ as her Savior yet, she was still being used by God. Her constant scrutiny of my lifestyle was a bit of a pain, especially for someone who had not yet fully surrendered. I pointed out to her countless situations where we had done this or done that to help others. Whenever you give justification, it is a strong sign you are not all in for Jesus. Little did either of us know that my excesses were going to become significantly more intense.

Had I heeded the warnings from my daughter and my wife about my escalating selfishness, the following chapters would be quite different. Unfortunately, I always wanted to do things in a bigger and more impressive way. I could try to act humble, but my actions and purchases were screaming, "Look at me!" I feel embarrassed talking about some of the foolish things I did. I describe these follies only to emphasize the error of my ways. In no way, shape or form do I deserve the grace and mercy that God has given me. *1 Peter 1:3 NKJV: "Blessed be the God and father of our Lord Jesus Christ, who according to his abundant mercy has begotten us again to a living hope through the resurrection of Jesus Christ from the dead."*

CHAPTER 5

——

MY COMPANY WAS GENERATING MORE REVENUE THAN
it ever had, though I was working fewer than ten hours a
week on-site. I did build a few machines at my little workshop at home, but for the most part, I worked on the trails
and did whatever I wanted. This meant that any time I
wanted to have a few drinks, there was nothing preventing
me from doing so. Amazingly, my health was pretty good,
considering that for decades I had stood on cement for
twelve to sixteen hours a day, working on equipment. Punishment did take its toll in some areas. My right knee was
painful most of the time, and the rest of my body was rid-
dled with arthritis. Sciatica was also an issue that I had to
contend with.

Self-medication, as long I controlled it, seemed reasonable. But the reality was that I overdid just about everything
I was involved in, whether it was drugs, alcohol or work. The
need to be successful always edged out my other bad behaviors. Now, it was no longer an issue. Success happened every
day without my input. Frequently, I would drink three or
four times a week, but not to the point of drunkenness as I
once did. But certainly, it impaired my judgment. I knew it

was just a matter of time before my drinking would cause problems for me.

God intervened in an interesting way. I went to the hospital to visit a man who worked at our company. He had fallen at home and sustained a serious head injury. When I visited him, he was making erratic jerking motions. In the hallway, his wife explained that he was going through withdrawal from alcohol. She said he was drinking a half-gallon every two days. I used to have drinks with him.

A year or so earlier, I saw him at a market picking up a half-gallon of Captain Morgan's. He seemed embarrassed to see me, and I could not figure out why. When I returned to my vehicle, I had the sense that he had an alcohol problem. I figured maybe he goes through a half-gallon once a month. According to his wife, he had a drinking problem for quite some time. As it turns out, she did also. To this day, I am not sure if they have been set free or not. I pray they both find deliverance.

When I saw him twitching on the bed, I had two thoughts. The first was that this could be me someday, and the second was that I needed to stop drinking so that I could be a silent support for this man. So now it has been nearly four years since I have had a drop of alcohol. Unfortunately, because of my addictive personality, it was just a matter of time before I turned to something else to take its place. For nearly my entire adult life, I was addicted to success, attention and the need to prove that I was in control. In other words, I was a workaholic. That addiction had overpowered any other addictions, but now I did not have the responsibility or the need to continue to push myself so hard.

Marijuana had become legal for medical use in my home state. By contacting the right doctor, you could get a medical marijuana card for a stubbed toe, practically. With all the aches and pains I had, it was not hard to justify the need for it. Consulting God about this never even crossed my mind. After all, I was still in control of my life and had managed to do okay. At this time, I had not yet come to the point of understanding. Looking back at all these events, it is easy for me to see that God was involved. I was just too ignorant to realize it and give Him glory for it, but there was one situation for which I gave Him all the glory.

My son and his wife had been trying to get pregnant for several years. Finally, they were successful. She was twenty weeks along with a baby girl. Tragically, she had a miscarriage and lost the baby. On top of that, it happened on my son's birthday. I prayed a lot over that situation, even though I was not living a fully surrendered life. Then something incredible happened. The miscarriage had occurred two months before Christmas, when my son and his wife would be coming from Nashville to see us. I woke up on December 22, and the Holy Spirit said, "Go get a little outfit for a boy." I was like, "No way." I told my wife what had happened, and she said, "Are you crazy?" For the next two days, I could not stop thinking about it. Finally, I was obedient, and on December 24, I bought a baby-boy outfit. On the 25th, I gave it to my son and his wife. They looked at me with tears streaming down their cheeks and asked, "Why would you do this?" I told them that I had no choice. I did not know what it meant, since I was just being obedient.

A little over two years later, they called us down to

Nashville. When we arrived, they had a gift bag hanging on the door. Inside the bag was a blue-framed ultrasound image of a baby. A few months later, one day before my birthday, my grandson was born. God was loving and caring for me and my family, even though I was continually turning my back on Him.

Back to the past. After nearly twenty-two years of having nothing to do with marijuana, I decided, "What could it hurt?" *Proverbs 26:11 NKJV: "As a dog returns to his own vomit, so a fool repeats his folly."* My wife was extremely upset and uncomfortable with my choice. You see, we were considered pillars of the community, with solid Christian values. Drinking alcohol was easy to hide, and in many Christian circles, it was even acceptable. But in my wife's eyes, pot was a totally different category. Part of my rationale was always that I would rather be on the road with somebody who is high than somebody who is drunk. She did not buy into that philosophy.

The first time I took a couple puffs, I could feel something inside me vehemently opposed to it. I had never been so paranoid and afraid of losing my mind. The cognitive ability that God had restored now was a jumbled mess. My thoughts, once fluid and concise, had lost all coherency. I was worried that this was a curse God put on me because of my disobedience. After nearly six hours, the effects wore off. You would think that any reasonable person would have got the message. Unfortunately, my desire to reignite a habit that had been dormant for decades was too strong. Our selfish flesh has an uncanny ability to convince us of almost anything. *Romans 8:7–8 NKJV: "Because the carnal mind is enmity against God; for it is not subject to the law of God, nor indeed can be. So then, those who are in the flesh cannot please God."*

I waited a few days and thought maybe just one or two puffs would be more manageable. I could blame Satan or the flesh, but it does not matter; it was disobedience to God. But I was bound and determined to somehow make it work. I kept trying different amounts and types, but I could not seem to get the right combination. The reality was that God just did not want me to do it. Occasionally, I would try to work on projects in my home shop after using pot. The effect it had on my engineering mind was staggering.

I had always enjoyed a degree of clarity that baffled many. However, under the influence of marijuana, I could do only the simplest repetitive task without freaking out. I had been able to find a solution to just about any engineering challenge I had encountered over the years, but in my altered state, I feared that I could not finish a project. Routinely, design parameters became huge stumbling blocks. Fortunately, after experiencing this problem only a couple of times, I realized something had to change.

I enjoyed the ability to juggle multiple projects simultaneously without stress. For whatever reason (God's blessing) my mind embraced multi-tasking. In fact, I felt stressed when I had nothing to do. My desire for clarity of mind outweighed my wanting to get high. I mentioned my dilemma to some other pot smokers, and they told me the THC level was much higher than it was twenty years ago. They recommended edibles, because the effects were more on the body and less on the mind. Still being in the driver's seat of my life, I figured, "What the heck, why not?"

I had someone make up some marijuana butter and use it to make brownies for me. The first time that I tried it, I knew I was on to something much better. I systematically would eat a brownie and try a different task. The paranoia and uneasiness with my engineering abilities were diminished considerably. I thought, "This may be a very good alternative." Through this whole process, I never once consulted God or asked what He thought. That is what an uncommitted and un-surrendered person does. Satan was thoroughly enjoying the decisions I was making. I even considered growing my own marijuana. When I told my wife about my plans, she could hardly believe her ears. She made as strong a stand as she could against this idea. At that point, it did not matter what she said, because I always did what I wanted.

By the grace of God, it never went that far. Looking back now, I find it nearly impossible to believe that I even considered growing pot plants. I believe this was a catalyst for what happened over the next nine months. My attitude of "I am going to do stuff, spend money, and draw attention to myself however I want" ruled my life. All of my actions were meant to make gains for my personal kingdom. You would think that after all the years of selfish behavior it could not get much worse. Please understand, I am not saying these things to draw attention to myself. I am simply revealing the foolish and selfish nature that I demonstrated.

We had lived in our house for more than twenty years. In that time, there was one partial repaint of a couple of rooms and some flooring changes. My wife and I decided that it was time for a remodel. What started out modestly ended up being costlier than building a new house. We probably put more money into the master bathroom than people spend on a small house. And we spent more money on furniture than I care to admit. Of course, we had to have a new deck, new siding, and a fancy new roof, plus hickory floors throughout most of the house, except for the kitchen and bathrooms. Those had sedimentary rocks quarried from the ocean. And every cabinet had quiet-close mechanisms on the doors and drawers. This is only a short list of our ridiculous spending.

That was just the start. I tripled the size of my work area/helicopter hangar. We added commercial bathrooms and a kitchen and created a designated space that could accommodate a few hundred people. Now I could entertain more people and have a larger group to brag to. Of course, this is all under the guise of our opening a youth adventure facility. There was some sincere merit in my thoughts concerning that project, but a significant degree of it was, "How can I justify spending nearly $2 million on all this unnecessary stuff?" I also bought a Bobcat skid steer with nearly a dozen attachments for it, plus other equipment I wanted. I made other guilt offerings to assuage my conscience, but because I didn't have a pure heart, they had no value.

The money that our manufacturing company was bringing in continued to feed my insatiable hunger for more, and these purchases were only the appetizers. The main course of vanity and self-promotion was yet to be served.

A few times throughout my life, I had been around people who had achieved fame. I attempted to launch my own TV show at two or three different times in my life. We would shoot a pilot episode and then pitch it. Ironically, many similar shows ended up on TV. I was like a washed-up actor making a last-ditch effort to grab the spotlight. The problem was, I had never achieved enough celebrity status to even be washed up. When people are full of themselves, arrogance and pride rule, and they think they can force anything to happen.

Having access to significant funds, I could do everything in a big way. I hired a producer and two camera operators and purchased equipment to begin the filming process. Filming one show at a time just was not enough, so we worked on two. One of them was going to be called *Mad Machinist* and the other *Speed My Drive*. I will go into more detail about these endeavors just so you can fully understand the depth of my foolishness.

One of the buildings we added during the expansion process was centered at the end of a nearly quarter-mile-long driveway. In an attempt to make *Speed My Drive* an eclectic show, we did some design features on the building. The show would revolve around our driving a collection of fast cars as fast as we could down driveways of different lengths. Of course, the longer the driveway, the more interesting and the better, so I removed an aging but suitable blacktop driveway and replaced it with a much more expensive concrete one. Not only that, I installed two fourteen-foot doors on opposite sides of the new building so that I would be able to drive straight through it and onto the forty-foot runoff pad on the other side.

For the first episode, I had a plan that my passenger did not know about. I was going to act as though the brakes were not functioning and crash through the building, with the cameras rolling. Of course, beforehand, we would install fake Styrofoam doors that looked real. I calculated that we could enter the building at close to seventy miles an hour. I would have to exercise perfect braking technique so that the vehicle would not travel beyond the cement pad behind the building. For someone as full of himself as I was, this seemed easy.

Obviously, this idea had great potential for calamity. Before the building was completed, I would blast down the driveway at nearly one hundred miles an hour, slam on the brakes at the last second, and hope that my calculations were accurate. Every run was like Russian roulette. When was the spinning cylinder going to land on the loaded chamber? God was trying to warn me, even early on. *John 16:13 NKJV: "However, when He, the Spirit of truth, has come, He will guide you into all truth; for He will not speak on His authority, but whatever He hears He will speak; and He will tell you things to come."* I had thoughts of crashing through the building and someone's child darting in front of the doorway during the filming process

Instead of sharing those thoughts with anyone, I instead emphasized the degree of safety that we needed to exercise. Meanwhile, I was eating marijuana-infused brownies on a regular basis. Not only was I attempting to do really stupid stuff, I was doing so in an altered state.

Naturally, for *Mad Machinist*, our other show, I was going to be the main character, and it would showcase all the crazy things I had built and would build. A majority of the filming took place in the barn initially. We were working on our first zip line at the time, so we would record different stages of testing and the manufacturing of the different components we needed to make it operational.

I had a complete machine shop at home and could make just about anything. When I needed something, I would buy it, even if I used it only once every year or two. The car collection that I had begun to assemble was about to take some drastic leaps forward. I had several nice vehicles that would have made anybody happy. I purchased a brand-new Tesla P85D and a Mercedes-Benz GTS. You could buy a dozen normally priced cars for what these two cost. My gluttonous behavior of feasting on whatever my flesh desired had caused me to become morbidly obese with worldly things. I had allowed myself to become almost completely occupied with things of this world.

This was the point where God began to show me how deeply saddened He was by my choices. When I bought the GTS without telling my wife, I knew I was going against God's will. When we try to do something in secret, it is almost always an indicator that we should not do it at all. Of course, I justified the purchase by telling myself, "It costs about the same as your Tesla." The reality was, I bought the Tesla because I wanted to be cool, but I spun it off as being my wife's car. After all, she was the one who usually drove it. She was always fine with just an average vehicle and was never into showboating like I was. She despised the looks and questioning she got whenever she drove the Tesla. I must admit, when I drove the GTS, I felt out of place and embarrassed.

I was a guy in my late-fifties driving a rough-riding, high-horsepower attention-getter just to pacify my ego. God knew I was incapable of restraining my carnality. On top of all this, I was trying to get my medical approval back so I could start flying again. I really wanted to have a helicopter for filming purposes and locating more driveways for *Speed My Drive*. This process would actually become part of the show: We would land at peoples' houses and try to get permission to use their driveway. Of course, we would get the permission ahead of time, so the discussions would be staged.

My daughter constantly reminded me how excessive and unnecessary my purchases were. She understandably would be embarrassed to have people come to our house. I picked her up from school one day in the GTS, and she sunk down in the seat like a baby kangaroo in its mother's pouch. She did not want anybody to see here, and within ten seconds of her being in the car, someone texted her about our flashy ride. She was not very happy with me. This was the first week of June, and school was nearly out. Father's Day was just around the corner, and I had not bought anything for myself in more than a week, so it was time for something.

CHAPTER 6

———

I HOPE I HAVE MADE IT CLEAR THAT THE PROPHETIC vision I had over twenty years ago was about to come true. Satan had continued to occupy more and more space inside my being. Remember my dream, the one in which Satan was leaning back into my head when I was calling out for Jesus? I had allowed that to happen because I did not feast on God's Word and have a surrendered relationship to Jesus Christ. Instead, I was like a Hoover vacuum cleaner, sucking up as much of the world as I could contain. You can tell by my pattern of consumption that even if I had everything, I would never have enough. I was like a heroin addict going from one fix to another. That is why it is so important for us to fill ourselves daily with God's Word and His presence. *Colossians 3:2 NKJV: "Set your mind on things above, not on things on the earth."* I was holding on to the thread of hope that since I had accepted Jesus as my Savior, all my sins were forgiven. That in itself is true, but unrepentant, willful sinning is not covered.

Sunday, June 21, was Father's Day. I had a large pile of brush that needed to be disposed of. We had cleared out several trees for the recent construction of new buildings and a large parking lot. My intention was to have an adventure park for youth groups and others. The idea was one-hundred percent mine, and I never consulted God. That was a huge mistake. The sky was blue, the sun was coming up on the horizon, and the birds were chirping. The morning was gorgeous, and it was a great day to be outside working. The night before, my daughter had inquired about going to Cedar Point the next day. I had undergone knee-replacement surgery eight weeks earlier and was experiencing a wonderful recovery. As with everything else, I pushed myself hard before surgery for physical strength and actually walked out of the hospital the day after my knee replacement. I wanted to get the projects cleaned up and finished.

The new buildings were completed, except for the new hangar. I had been trying for quite some time to get the FAA to approve my medical certificate. There was not much sense in cutting a huge opening for a door in the building that was going to be the hangar if it would never be used. I had been rejected by the FAA probably six times at this point. Flying helicopters was great fun but also just another way of showing off. This will go down in history as one of the most memorable Father's Days for me.

I just want to say first and foremost this next incident was one-hundred percent my fault. Never, ever, ever, ever use gasoline to start fires. With that said, I will explain what happened. I grew up on a farm where clearing fields and fence rows was a common practice. Many times, I witnessed my father and others start fires using gasoline, always with great caution to avoid a disaster. I had successfully done the same thing at least a dozen times. That particular morning, I had a huge cautionary sense in my spirit. In my whole lifetime I never had felt that way. I had the sense that something was going to go very wrong with this gasoline. That morning, I continued with my plan, but with a more cautious approach to lighting the fire.

I grabbed a branch that was maybe eight feet long. After retrieving an old rag from the shop, I wrapped it around the end of the branch. I poured some gasoline on one end of the brush pile and then the rag. Standing several feet from the brush pile, I ignited the rag on the end of the stick, then I lit the brush pile. Everything went as planned, with no problems. Grabbing the can of gasoline, I moved to the other side of the brush pile, at least fifty feet away from it. Because of the distance, I thought there would be no chance of any ambers or sparks reaching me. The five-gallon gas can was about half full. I looked around and enjoyed the cool summer morning just a few seconds too long.

When I heard a *whoosh* sound, I knew I was in big trouble. My legs were entangled in tree branches. The branches were doused in gasoline, and I was holding a can with two gallons of highly flammable accelerant. I had serious reservations that I would survive much beyond the ignition point. The first thought I had was, "If I try to step backward I will surely fall and cover myself in more gasoline." No scenario I could imagine was the least bit hopeful. This is why I had a warning planted deep inside me. Why would God try to warn me when I had been so selfish and self-centered with everything that I did? *1 Timothy 2:3-4 NKJV: "For this is good and acceptable in the sight of God our Savior, who desires all men to be saved and to come to the knowledge of the truth."*

If I died on Father's Day, it would forever taint that day for my family. But at that point, there was nothing I could do to change that possibility. The first wave of heat began to penetrate the top layers of my skin, the pain registering in my brain. Like an avalanche, the heat was uncontrollable and unpredictable. What started as a single sensation now had the collective energy of a stampede. Just as the situation was reaching a point of no return, something happened.

I have pondered this memory for a couple of years now. There is no rational explanation. No matter how hard I try, I cannot seem to step away from this reality. Through the orange flames and crackling sounds, I witnessed a streak of light descending from the east, then a glowing face inches from mine. My next memory is of lying on my back nearly thirty feet away from where I was. I was beside a gravel pile. As I looked down at the smoldering skin that was beginning to detach from my legs, I pondered these questions: "What happened to the burning can of gas that was in my hand? How did I get out of the tangled web of tree branches? Why was I not on fire anymore? How was I transported thirty feet instantaneously?"

Looking at the burning pile of brush, I could see the gas can belching out large plumes of fire. Milliseconds earlier, I had been trapped in that inferno. For whatever reason, my encounter with death was supernaturally postponed. That reality did not fully set in until after my evaluation at the University of Michigan burn center. The newly renovated house, new cars, new buildings, new zip lines, new equipment, and filming of potential TV shows did not enter my mind. The intense firing of nerve receptors started as a trickle but almost instantly became a torrent. There was no way to escape the blistering pain.

Before I went to the hospital, a text notification on my cell phone momentarily distracted me. Protected in my pocket, the phone was still functioning. When I reached in my pocket and retrieved the phone, a large chunk of skin came off the top of my hand. At that point, I am sure, the shock began to set in. It was 8:28 a.m. The text was from a friend wishing me a happy Father's Day. Millions of nerve receptors were prompting my brain to do something quickly, but instead, I responded, "Same to you, buddy. Have a great day." Nearly a month later, I told my friend that a few seconds before his text, I had burned all the skin off both legs between my knees and ankles.

The house was a few hundred yards away. I was dirty and sweaty and could not imagine going to the ER in this condition. I delicately got up and walked a few feet to my utility vehicle.

The majority of my life, I considered myself a pretty tough guy. I had run drill bits through my hand, gotten stitched up several times, smashed fingers and toes, and had just gone through a knee replacement with hardly any complaining. Getting burned this severely was a totally different experience. Now I was learning what pain really was. Imagine the first time that you were burned, say on a fingertip. The wound blistered up, and you felt discomfort for a while. Well, take that discomfort and multiply it by a factor of several thousand and you will understand the magnitude of the situation.

As I walked into the house, I called my wife's name and

said, "I think we are going to need to go to the hospital." She could tell by the smell and my appearance that this was serious. Not being one who can handle stressful situations, especially when it comes to bodily harm, she instantly went into panic mode. She was not happy with me when I told her I was going to take a shower before we went. I could not imagine lying on the gurney all sweaty and smelly.

When the water from the showerhead trickled down my legs, the pain nearly brought me to my knees. Thick layers of skin were already separating, leaving the nerve endings exposed. It was like hot lava coursing down a mountainside. Every little crack and crevice that the water entered caused excruciating pain. I began shaking uncontrollably. Quickly, I finished in the shower, carefully got dressed, and called the same brother I called the day of my heart attack. He later joked that he was not going to answer the phone the next time I called him on a Sunday.

After explaining my situation, he said I should go to the hospital's burn unit, where the doctors specialized in such large-scale burns. Any place else would just transfer me there anyway. Calling an ambulance would have been a far better decision, but instead my wife, daughter and I attempted the patient delivery on our own. I was in a great deal of pain, and my wife was very nervous. I took a cold, wet washcloth with us to help ease the pain, but every time I moved it from one spot on my leg to another, a big glob of skin would come with it. With the nerve endings exposed, just a slight breeze from the AC spiked the pain level.

The journey took us about an hour. We had stopped at a smaller hospital on the way to see if I could get something for the pain. They suggested we go to the University of Michigan burn center. They offered to call an ambulance but indicated it might be faster if we drove ourselves. As soon as we arrived at the burn center, they rushed me inside, began evaluating my injuries, and gave me massive doses of pain medication. One of the more uncomfortable procedures involved inserting a small camera into my throat and lungs to see how much damage was done.

I have always had a raspy voice, but when they heard it, the doctors were concerned that I might have suffered severe internal injuries from inhaling fire. After the internal inspection was finished, one of the doctors grabbed my right hand and marveled, "It is amazing that you had the wherewithal to cover your mouth."

I responded, "I did no such thing."

"Yes, you did," he said. "I can tell by the burn patterns on your nose and hand."

He showed me how I had cupped my hand around my mouth and nose, leaving a gap between my thumb and forefinger. That gap allowed the tip of my nose to be burned.

"That was what saved your life, my friend," the doctor said.

The other odd thing that the doctor commented on was the burn pattern on my legs. "Normally, most burns come from one direction," he said. "You are burned completely around both legs. It appears as if someone pulled you right out of a fire."

Little did he know that was true.

These facts are just more confirmation of the supernatural event that took place. Think about the sequence of events. The burning gas can is dropped, my mouth and nose are covered with my hand, and I leap straight up and out of the fire to land thirty feet away. What do you think the probability is of an untrained civilian being able to respond like that? What do you think the chances are of a twenty-year-veteran firefighter doing such a thing? No matter how long I ponder the event, the only conclusion I come to is that this was supernatural.

Once the examination was completed, the doctors gave me even more drugs to put me in a twilight state. They would have to remove all of the burned skin so that they could do skin-grafting. The fact that I was lying on the ground with large open wounds made them very concerned about infection, so they had to vigorously clean the wounds. Three times over the course of the next week, I was put under and scrubbed hard. This delayed the skin-grafting many days beyond what was intended.

I knew I was in a crucial situation, and I was praying that God would be with me. Somehow I knew in my heart that this was a wake-up call. Watching how hard the nurses worked and what they had to put up with made me choose a direction. I was going to try to be a model patient and be very thankful for their care. On top of that, I sensed the power of many people praying for me. Never in my life had I experienced that. I requested that I not have any visitors. The daily dose of a dozen OxyContin pain pills had reduced a strong-willed, independent man to a paranoid little boy.

The OxyContin kept me in an altered, twilight state. In fact, at one point, I had a bizarre reaction. Since the University of Michigan was a teaching hospital, students participated in procedures and other learning opportunities. Unbeknown to me, I was the subject of a panel review. Apparently, the things I was talking about during my drug-induced psychosis were quite peculiar. One of the students said it was as if there was a consciousness trying to separate itself from my body, almost as if my spirit was trying to escape a drug-induced prison. A few other people came up to me when I regained consciousness and said they had never seen anything so strange.

I had a puzzling sensitivity to certain things. Obviously, I was able to tolerate marijuana-infused cookies and brownies. Heavier substances seemed to unhinge my delicate balance. During my time in the hospital, I did not partake in anything that the hospital did not prescribe for me. There were a couple of nights I had my wife stay in the hospital with me, because I felt like a small child: very paranoid and afraid. That was a shock to me after I had spent decades as the CEO of multiple companies. I rarely was afraid of anything, but fear now surrounded me, like the air that I breathed, and there was no way to get away from it.

Finally, on the seventh day, the doctors determined that the infection was under control, so they could begin the skin-grafting procedures. They informed me that I would be put into two temporary leg casts. Because my legs were burned all the way around, there were not enough anchor points for the grafting. They wanted to be sure that the skin would have enough time to adhere without moving, so they used about seventy-five staples per leg to keep the skin in place.

When someone is in the hospital for an extended period

of time, they get to know the staff a little. From their appearances and conversation, I could tell which staff members were Christians and which were not. Even though I was in a heavily sedated state, I prayed and thought about God quite a bit. The staff complimented me about my attitude. They said how much better it was to have a positive attitude and faith. I am sure I spent more time talking to God and praying than I had in years.

The burn unit staff allowed me to dress my own wounds, so early on in my stay, I was removing my own bandages. The nurses commented that they had never seen anybody do it so soon. I was determined to get out as soon as I could. Not only was I a prisoner in my drug-induced mind, but the surroundings were closing in on me, draining the life right out of me, from my perspective. There were so many more burn patients who were far, far worse off than I was.

Though twenty-five percent of my body had sustained third-degree burns, but they were in ideal locations. The doctors grafted skin from my back and thighs, which meant more staples and painful recovery. In my case, full mobility and minimal scarring made the burns somewhat of an invisible injury.

You would think that after going through this, I would reevaluate my life. Unfortunately, my selfish ways continued. I returned home several days sooner than expected, and we had arranged for a nurse to come to the house and assist me. Because I had become skilled with my own bandages, she came only twice to observe me. She gave me her stamp of approval and I continued the recovery process. The massive remodel of the house had just been completed.

The first opportunity I had to enjoy it was not entertaining at all. In a few short weeks, I had become dependent on OxyContin. Ironically, the pharmacy messed up the prescription, and I went twenty-five hours without any pain meds. This was far more challenging for me psychologically then it was physically. The little boy who had emerged in me was afraid if my wife left the room. She made the mistake of going outside and burning the trash right next to the pile of brush where I had been burned. This filled me with panic. The clarity of mind that I had maintained for twenty-five years was slipping away.

When we finally got the prescription filled, I told my wife that I would cut the dosage in half every four hours until I was off of it. A day and a half later, I was finished with the OxyContin. The pain was significant, but a return to clarity of mind was far more important to me. A few nights into this stage of the recovery, I was awake around 1 a.m. The massive burns were constantly seeping body fluids, so we had to put plastic covers on the bed. I woke up and walked around a bit. I can remember crying out to God, "Please Lord, restore my mind. Please Lord, get me through this."

I distinctly remember His answer being implanted in my spirit: "You are a warrior of my kingdom. You will be called to duty and face far greater things than this." He went on to say, "You will be fine. This is nothing. I am with you." *2 Corinthians 4:7–11 NKJV: "But we have this treasure in earthen vessels, that the excellence of the power may be of God and not of us. We are hard pressed on every side, yet not crushed, we are perplexed, but not in despair, persecuted, but not forsaken, struck down, but not destroyed always carrying about in the body the*

dying of the Lord Jesus, that the life of Jesus also may be mani-
fested in our body. For we who live are always delivered to death
for Jesus sake, that the life of Jesus also may be manifested in our
mortal flesh."

For me, this was a significant moment. I wish I could say it was the point where I turned to God and surrendered to him, but I was not quite there yet.

God had been continually trying to get my attention, and I had continually been ignoring him. My focus was almost fully on things of this world. I am sure God wondered what it would take to change that, and of course He knew, but I did not. Just a few weeks later, I found out how much I really pissed off God. Many of you may not like that term, but the title of this book was placed in me a few years ago. I did not know if I was ever supposed to write this book; there are many things revealed here that are not flattering.

Testimony of my ridiculously selfish behavior is intended to help anyone who has ventured on this path. The vast majority of people in the Western churches today are confronting similar issues. The very sad part about this is that many will never realize it. Until that switch is flipped in a person's spirit, and the fifty-one percent mark has been reached, there will never be in-depth understanding. The fifty-one percent I am referring to is the percentage of your life that you must surrender to Jesus, and surrendering one-hundred percent, of course, is full commitment. It is unrealistic to think that this will instantly take place. There is a process involved, and the Holy Spirit will show you what things you need to weed out of your life. How ironic that I would use that last phrase. Praise be to Jesus for working in our lives!

CHAPTER 7

————

ON JULY 18, A SATURDAY MORNING, MY DAUGHTER was gone for the weekend, and it was just my wife and I at home. I was running low on my supply of cookies and brownies infused with marijuana butter. Eating them left me in a mildly altered state, similar to the effect of drinking two alcoholic drinks. For me, it was more of a body relaxer and did not seem to affect my mind much. However, when I smoked pot, the sensation was much more intense. I pretty much stopped doing that because of the effects. Many times, I would not even mention to my wife that I had consumed some edibles. She was unaware of any behavioral changes. I even convinced her to try a little, but she did not like it, because it made her tired, with little or no other effect. She still did not like that I ate the brownies and cookies, but because they didn't leave the lingering smell that smoking pot did, she found it more tolerable. I had never had any marijuana in any form in my house, until this day. This was a huge mistake, I initially thought, but it was really a huge blessing.

Because my daughter was gone, I had bought some brownie and cookie mixes to make up a fresh supply that I planned to store in the refrigerator in my shop. Keep in mind that this whole time I *thought* I was a pretty serious Christian, but the bar is set so low in the United States that it does not take much to reach that level. After all, medical marijuana was legal, and I had just survived some pretty serious burns. One thing that mankind is good at is justification.

I started my cooking exercise around 9 a.m. By 10:45 a.m., I had finished most of it. Since my daughter was not around, I thought I would have a brownie and even offered some to my wife. She was reluctant but took a small bite. The effects were similar to what we had experienced in the past. She got tired and went to the bedroom and lay down, and I felt more relaxed and carefree. The clarity of mind that I enjoyed seemed to stay intact.

Just after 11 a.m., something came out of the bedroom and into the area where I was. Shock and concern do not begin to explain what I was feeling. I wondered if it was a demonic entity, because it never revealed its face to me. For the next forty-two minutes, I had quite the conversation. This spirit was very upset with decisions I had been making, even to the point that it would never make eye contact with me. I have never felt so disgusted with myself and humiliated by my own foolishness. This is my recollection of what was said, and I pray that God helps me not to mislead or deceive anyone with this experience in anyway.

The first words that the entity spoke were, "What is wrong with you? Your choices and decisions have been unbelievably foolish." These were followed by, "Who do you think you are, treating me as disrespectfully as you have?"

Then, "Do you know who I am? I have power over life and death." This was the introduction that I received, and these words were stated in a very commanding tone. Between each statement were focused comments pertaining to each.

My mind was racing, and my awareness of reality took a huge leap. I felt that something far beyond myself was now addressing me. The entity moved closer and was looking at its left arm and hand. Twisting its wrist back and forth, it said, "It feels so strong to be in a body." Its movements were beyond what we understand to be physically possible. My mind was trying to comprehend what my eyes were seeing.

Not knowing exactly what I was dealing with made me fearful and timid, which was very contrary to my normal disposition. *2 Corinthians 11:14 NKJV: "No wonder! For Satan himself transforms himself into an angel of light. Therefore it is no great thing if his ministers also transformed themselves into ministers of righteousness, whose end will be according to their works."*

So I asked, "Who are you?"

"I know everything about you, everything," the being said. "You have no right to ask me any questions."

The response shook me to my innermost being.

Pointing to the brownies and marijuana butter, it demanded, "How dare you bring this into your house that I have sanctified? I have been increasingly disturbed with your behavior. I have given you many warnings, and you reject them all. I tolerated you having this in your workshop, but I despised it, and you knew it. I will not tolerate it being in this house. In your actions, you chose to honor me not. I have allowed you to have everything your heart desires."

Even though the words were not spoken, the sense of greed and selfishness crashed down around me. The reality of who I really had been was being forced into focus.

The delineation continued. "Your mother is a very special spirit. There have been only a few like her throughout history. She was the seed that would lead to your daughter. I have very special plans for your daughter."

Then, pointing to the brownies, it said, "This source of deception can never, ever be around her. Her purity and innocence must be preserved. If you would have only consulted me instead of seeking your selfish desires, this could have been avoided. You do not understand how the doorways of evil are opened up, but I do. Have I made myself clear to you?"

The face and eyes were still shrouded in secrecy, but every voice inflection penetrated my being. Like the bullets from a firing squad, every word pierced me to my core. There was no escape.

I was fully aware of the fact that my mother had saintly qualities. This in turn led me to think about my father, who had passed away a few years earlier. The entity knew my thoughts without my speaking them. "Your father, he is doing fine, just plowing the fields in heaven," it said. There was almost a little chuckle, as if it knew my father personally. My father would oftentimes have funny little jokes and stories to share.

The truth about who I was speaking with was becoming clear. Still skeptical, I asked, "Please tell me, who are you?"

Walking over to the counter and picking up a Bible and lifting it into the air, the being proclaimed, "I am the Word, and this is my Word. You need to study the Word." *John 1:1*

NKJV: "In the beginning was the Word, and the Word was with God, and the Word was God."

The entity walked to the granite countertop, pointed to a spot that was illuminated by a sunbeam, and said, "Do you see this? This is a symbol that many use to refer to me, but to only a few does it truly have meaning. Do you see it?"

No matter how hard or from what angle I looked, it just was not apparent to me.

The entity pointed to it again. "There in front of you, how can you not see it?"

That was a strong indicator of my spiritual blindness. I am not sure if the entity was pointing at a cross, heart, fish or something else, but I did not see it.

At this point, I decided that I would ask as many questions as I could. The greedy part of me thought, "I bet you know the winning lottery numbers." I never uttered those words, but I did receive a response. "What is wrong with you? Why would you want to play the lottery? Do not play the lottery ever again."

The mere thought of the lottery filled the entity with disgust. I could tell that my lack of gratitude was a great concern, as it should be. The fact that the entity mentioned the lottery was not surprising. On rare occasions, my wife or I would purchase a lottery ticket. Obviously, God knew I was not even capable of handling the things we already had. He was revealing the condition of my heart, which was totally wrong. I was focused on the things of this world and not on Him. How much of a disgrace I had been was beginning to sink in.

"Did you save me from the fire?" I asked. The response

was silence. I asked the same question again. "Did you save me from the fire?" Again the response was silence. For the final time, I asked, "Did you or any of your angels or my guardian angel save me from the fire?" The response was silence. Still, I felt this entity had saved me, but I questioned the wisdom of doing so. The entity was definitely troubled by the thick-headed nature that I had demonstrated for so long.

What was even more concerning than this was that my stupidity was not over. This troubled awareness that I sensed from the entity was somewhere in the future. Before the next statements were made, it seemed to reflect on the decision to allow me to continue living. As I looked at the entity, it was as if all the actions for the rest of my life were fast-forwarding through its mind. I never could see the face or the eyes. The long hair on its head shrouded them.

I asked if it would look at me. The entity refused and was even perturbed at the thought. There was a point of awareness by the entity, however, where the frustration of my choices began to change direction. I had the sense that it detected a change in my priorities at some point in the future. This seemed to provide a spark of hope. Then the instructions continued.

"Never take a car and drive it through that building as a silly stunt. Does your foolishness and need for self-promotion ever end? Do you understand? A great disaster will happen if you try it even one time." The entity was referring to *Speed My Drive*, the TV project we were working on. Part of the show was to record people's expression as they were crashing through fake doors at high speed. This was a very dangerous proposition for sure. I already had concerns about it but chose to ignore them. This was one of those examples that God was referring to. He had tried to warn me on many occasions.

Other things happened during this encounter that I believe I am not supposed to mention. The description that I have given may seem nonchalant, but the experience was intense. The being had control over the physical world that I had never witnessed or imagined possible. To fully disclose my ridiculous behavior, I must report more.

What came out of that bedroom was visible but totally unidentifiable. I saw, heard or felt the voice, gestures, personality, mental acuity, physical strength and unnatural body motions. These were all things that I had never witnessed before. The essence of the physical form was my wife. This encounter would have been just as alien if it had been any other appearance. I cannot imagine a veteran actor pulling off a role like this. CGI or special effects would have been necessary. On top of that, we discussed certain things during the interaction that were unknown to my wife.

At the beginning of the encounter, I was trembling yet still an a-hole. I knew something was occupying my wife's body. I did not know if it was good or evil, but I had the audacity to think of sexual interaction. I even went as far as saying, "Maybe we should go in the bedroom and have some fun." In my polluted, carnal mind, I imagined what it might be like sexually with a possessed woman. *Galatians 5:19: "Now the works of the flesh are evident, which are adultery, fornication, uncleanness, lewdness."* All the while, I had been thinking I was a Christian.

For the record, it creeps me out to think I did such a thing. Hopefully, you are just as disgusted, because I was a filthy individual. As the interaction continued, it was like heaping hot coals on my head. The reality of who I was speaking with made me wish that I could hit the rewind button, or have a large mountain crash down on top of me.

When I realized it was the Authority of God, I became much more reverent and courteous in my conversation. "Where is my wife?" I asked.

The Authority replied, "She is with the others, and she doesn't know if she wants to come back."

With tears, I pleaded, "I love her and want her back."

The Authority said, "It is her choice if she returns."

"But are you not in control of that?" I asked.

"I am in control, since I gave her to you," said the Authority. "Now it is up to her. If she wants to return, she will. We should pray together for her return."

Then it motioned for me to move to the prayer bench that my wife and I used during our wedding. Kneeling beside me, it reached up with its arm in an unnatural way, as though the joints had become unhinged. This was the third time that I had noticed unnatural body movements that cannot be explained in the physical realm.

It didn't dawn on me that the Authority of God was asking me to pray beside Him, at least not in the sense that I could see physical evidence. I prayed that my wife would return to me. I committed to becoming a better husband. I said that I would read the Word more. I requested for Jesus to change me. I promised to be a better father to my daughter. I vowed that I would be a protector and keep her away from certain influences. I promised that I would never touch marijuana in any form again, ever. I begged for the opportunity to do things right.

The Authority got up and declared, "It is time for me to leave." Practically in a streak of light, it disappeared toward the bedroom. I scurried in behind and could not believe what I was seeing. My wife was lying on the bed, sleeping peacefully, with nothing moved or out of place. I stood there for several minutes, just staring at her. Finally, she woke up, smiled at me, and asked, "Is everything okay?"

I am sure she had never seen such a puzzled look on my face before. "Do you know what just happened?" I asked.

She looked around the bedroom as if she had missed something obvious. Then she said, "No, I am just waking up, I guess. For how long was I sleeping?"

Nearly an hour had elapsed by this point. I explained to her in great detail what happened. She was baffled and unable to explain what transpired. At the most, she may have had some foggy imprints in her mind. She was like a bystander watching a scenario unfold before her. Sketchy, fragmented details were all she could offer. She had no coherent memory of the event. She was disturbed at just the thought of something occupying her consciousness. Eventually, she refused to talk about it anymore.

I had never before been so unsettled. The true nature of the horrendous person I had been was exposed before me in vivid detail. The sense of utter worthlessness and shame was like quicksand swallowing me with every thought that I had. I was this puffed-up man inflated by my own ego now forced me to see myself the way God did. For once in my life, I was humbled to the point of change. Unfortunately, though I could finally catch a glimpse of the change I needed, my sinful nature was too strong to be overcome just yet. *1 Corinthians 2:14 NKJV: "But the natural man does not receive the things of the Spirit of God, for they are foolishness to him, nor can he know them, because they are spiritually discerned."*

Though some details of this experience cut so deeply in my soul that they caused instant change, many of my characteristics remained unchecked for quite some time. As unbelievable as it may seem, God was not willing to give up on me.

I was not sure that I should continue writing about my experiences, so I had a good friend read what I had written so far. He questioned my description of the spiritual entity. I pondered this question before writing and came to an initial conclusion on my own. I remembered a Scripture about testing the Holy Spirit, so during the encounter, I had asked, "Did Jesus come in the flesh?" The response was, "Yes, of course." When I specifically asked, "Who are you?" the response was the Word. I assumed that it was Jesus, but at the exact time I was responding to my friend, my daughter came into the office. She had just edited Chapter 7 and said, "I believe it was the Holy Spirit, because I felt something when I read it." I thought that the timing of her saying this was amazing. I questioned her in more details, yet she was unable to give more clarity.

I later added these last two paragraphs of this chapter. My desire is to give total disclosure of everything that happened as the story unfolds. I had initially written that the entity was Jesus. Clarification on this issue is very important, since that was a conclusion I reached on my own. I do believe that the response concerning Jesus coming in the flesh was sufficient evidence that the messenger was of God. The sense that I currently have is that it was the Authority of God. That is how I rephrased my human understanding of what occurred. Above all things, bringing glory and honor to God is my only desire.

CHAPTER 8

————

A SIGNIFICANT EVENT OCCURRED AFTER I WROTE
Chapter 7. It could be the whole reason I was compelled by
God to start writing the story. I believe it makes the most
sense to insert it here so that the event I just described can
be more easily correlated.

I have a great deal more to share about the process of
God showing me who I really was. Consequently, my understanding of God is vastly different from what it was when
this occurred. I have had the time to grow in the Lord and
understand His ways, and I can hear the Holy Spirit far
more clearly. I wrote Chapter 7 at a time when my wife and
I were having a disagreement. On top of that, a spiritual
question concerning adultery was on my mind: Because this
was my second marriage, was my wife committing adultery
with me?

When the Lord had fully awakened me to the true nature of my fallen condition, my desperate search began. The
reality of living a life of unrepentant sin and doing as I
pleased finally was burdening my soul. So many years had
been lost to the insignificant things of this world. I am not
sure if I ever truly experienced the fear of the Lord, and this

was the result. *Proverbs 28:14 NKJV: "Happy is the man who is always reverent, but he who hardened his heart will fall into calamity."* Now that my spiritual eyes were more open, the Holy Spirit was exposing my shortcomings and teaching me what I ought to learn. Things that were once covered were now revealed.

My wife and I demonstrated love toward each other for the most part, but when it came to disagreements, it was always my way or the highway. I was burdened by my very selfish and dominant position and definitely was not Christ-like. She has a submissive and peaceful nature that I took advantage of. She always knew that I could out-argue her, and there was not much sense in trying to win a dispute with me.

I would set up situational traps in our communication, or purposely ask questions of a leading nature. It was straight-up personal manipulation to always make myself look and feel superior and smarter than she was. If I ever did acknowledge any wrongdoing, I would justify it somehow. "I support you," or "Look at all the long hours I work." Or the worst one of all, "Just about any woman in the world would trade positions with you." You could pick a variety of chauvinistic and descriptive statements to degrade my character, and probably all of them would apply. I cannot even joke about this behavior, because it is completely inexcusable.

Keep in mind, these events took place eighteen months after the visitation by the Authority of God. I will continue to describe those eighteen months once I make this declaration of God's power. I started to take to heart how a husband is to treat his wife. Starting with our twenty-eighth year of marriage, we had deeper, more transparent communications than ever before. I would specifically dedicate time, patience and self-control to keep my mouth closed in order to learn more about my wife. God sent me on a journey, prior to this revelation, to learn how to have compassion for people. My compassion for humankind grew more in forty-two days than it had in nearly forty-two years of adult life.

Because God showed me I can love humanity the way He does, I should easily be able to love my wife the way Jesus wants me to. *Ephesians 5:25 NKJV: "Husbands, love your wives, just as Christ also loved the church and gave himself for her."* We were able to talk about tough subjects in a peaceful and respectful way while allowing input from each other. Through this transition period, my wife gained confidence that our marriage was stronger than ever, but then God put me to the test. For six days, I thought I was going to have to sacrifice something precious to me. I could not believe that the Holy Spirit was prompting me to examine my heart concerning adultery.

For several days, I pored over Scripture and watched hours of YouTube videos. The adultery that I am describing had been going on ever since I met my second wife. The Bible is clear on marriage, and I am very cautious as I relay this story. Divorcing my first wife was wrong and never should have happened. I can give you all kinds of justifications. That is about the only skill man possesses on his own. The adultery I am referring to was continuous with my second wife. I had great fear that my actions were going to cause her to go to hell. Of course, I would be going with her. I could not believe that after all we had been through, and having a sixteen-year-old daughter, God would want me to divorce her. I believe God was testing me. "Are you all in or not?"

After many days of trembling before the Lord, I broke the news to my wife. We had gone through the previous months together deepening our understanding of and commitment to each other. This fortified our relationship enough for her not to freak out when she heard what I had to say. She was calm about it and left it up to me to decide. "If you really think that is what the Holy Spirit is telling you to do," she said, "I have to trust you." At that point, God knew that I had raised the knife as much as Abraham did with Isaac. I now fully understood what it meant to fear the Lord. *Genesis 22:12 NKJV: "And he said, do not lay your hand on the lad, or do anything to him, for now I know that you fear God, since you have not withheld your son, your only son, from me."* God is in control of all things, and anything short of full surrender has no value.

Through revelation in the Scripture, the testing was over a few days later. I am not going to mention the reason for my release. I will give no excuse to justify divorce. Do not do it. Any fewer details than what I just gave would not make much sense. I needed to establish the dilemma that God put before me concerning my second wife. There is a much closer correlation to Abraham's situation than meets the eye. God asked me to kill my marriage, as a test of my faith, and ultimately I would have been obedient to that.

Abraham had faith because God told him that his descendants would be more numerous than the stars. Likewise, during my visitation, Jesus told me that he had given me my current wife. Had I remembered that, I would not have anguished so much over the situation. Jesus had already established the fact that he blessed her to me. The day before I wrote about the visitation I watched another video. The subject matter was about remarriage and adultery. Once again, this issue troubled me. Was it Satan just throwing stuff up in my mind to get me off track? I could not understand why God would bring it up again.

The instant that the words appeared on the paper in front of me, it was like, "Hallelujah!" I had such a huge sense of relief: The burden of doubt was forever taken away by the Lordship of Jesus Christ. I am not implying anything by this. Do not get divorced. The timing of this chain of events took place with clockwork perfection. Only the creator of the universe could orchestrate such a phenomenon. Now for part two of the revelation, which exposes a far more shady and dark side. My wife and I had a reoccurring disagreement concerning sexual matters.

For nearly three years, I could not understand the change in her behavior. Our intimacy with one another had always been enjoyable and engaging for both of us. Her interest level and desire dropped to near zero. Many of you may think it was due to her age, and maybe the onset of menopause. This was not the case. Initiation on her behalf was practically nonexistent. She was submissive and did seem to receive equal enjoyment once I initiated sex. The problem was that the frequency seemed to be an ongoing issue for her. That had never come up in the past. Not only that, it was beginning to feel like it was a burden for her.

Even by her own admittance, I was treating her better. I

was helping around the house more. We were having great conversations with equal input. I was giving her compliments, even when she did not want to receive them. Daily, I would tell her I loved her. I am not saying these things to show how great I was, because clearly, I was not. These are acknowledgments that she made on her own about my behavior.

A couple of times, she even thought some evil influence was causing her to act this way. She could not understand it. She would ask me to pray for her regarding this issue, because she did not want to deal with it anymore. From that, I knew her heart was sincere and that she detected the change herself. By this point, our walk with the Lord was the top priority for both of us. We did not want these distractions to continue to cause our focus to drift, even in the least. Also, we knew as husband and wife we were one flesh. Unity was paramount for a strong front.

The same day I had watched the video concerning remarriage and adultery, I also wrote about another part of the visitation, describing the most embarrassing, deviant behavior you could imagine. Just to reiterate, this creeps me out to even talk about it. Prior to my full understanding of the entity that occupied my wife's body, I had propositioned it. I was fully aware that some type of manifestation had taken over her. I suggested that we should go into the bedroom, knowing full well what my intentions were. To this very moment, I am disgusted with myself many times over. There is one other very interesting aspect I need to share.

The day that my daughter and I returned home from a two-day road trip, my wife had a good friend over the house who also attended our spiritual study group. I knew they were very close and probably had talked about most issues. After my daughter went upstairs, I asked a question: "So how well do you guys think you know each other?" The friend said, "Pretty good, I think." Then I blurted out, "So you have probably talked about sex and frequency and stuff like that." My wife said, "Wow, just jump in there with the big questions." They both chuckled.

I was not as lighthearted about it, because this issue seemed to be recurring. We would talk, pray and read the Bible, and seemingly come to a solution. Inevitably the issue would rise to the surface once again. Our young friend, probably half our age, detected a wedge between us. She definitely has spiritual wisdom far beyond her years. She told me, in front of my wife, "Something is off between you two, and I think it is caused by you." Surprisingly, I restrained my desire to respond in the flesh and instead considered her words. She was right, but I could have guessed a thousand reasons why and not hit on the right one.

Putting this story down on paper has taken quite some time. For the most part, I was left to discern the reality of the visitation myself. I did talk to a couple ministers who I knew. Both believed that something supernatural did occur. Conversations that my son and I had were very methodical and deliberate. The most important thing was asking God to show me the truth behind this, but there was one hinge pin that started the process. I insisted that my wife give me an answer.

Repeatedly, she refused to talk about it. She said that whatever happened was between me and God. She had practically no recollection of anything. Regardless, undeniable things appeared and were spoken of that could be explained only by a supernatural presence. I explained to her that maybe the situation did not affect her but that it was life-changing for me. I begged, "I have to know. Was any of that you?" She did not answer. Through the night, she had spent several hours praying. She told me the next morning, "You can consider it God talking to you." I knew beyond a shadow of a doubt the very day it happened that it was God. I had to be sure. I had too much to answer for already. I did not want to add any more to the list. The very day she told me that, I began to write.

When I finished writing Chapter 7, God made two issues very clear to me. One, He granted me my current wife. This issue is resolved forever, and a great sense of relief came over me. Two, I needed to ask my wife for forgiveness for propositioning her body when I clearly knew she was not in control. After you become fully surrendered, obedience to the Holy Spirit gets easier and easier. As soon as I finished the last sentence of Chapter 7, I went and got my wife. She didn't even know that I was writing about this journey. I told her that I just wrote about the visitation. I stated, "I only want you to respond to one request, please: Make sure to the best of your ability that I have absolutely no deception in the words that I wrote."

As she read, tears trickled down her cheeks. Her body movements and groans revealed her great discomfort. By the time she finished going through the words, she was nearly speechless. I asked her, "As far as you can tell, is there anything in there that is deceptive?"

She shook her head no. I was pretty sure that would be

her response. I was continually praying to God that I would not write anything that the Holy Spirit did not support. Several times, I had to remove sentences or re-word them extensively. Only when I felt as though I was getting a thumbs-up did I move on.

I told my wife that I had asked God for forgiveness for making the sexual proposition. Actually, the day that it happened, I addressed the issue. I never considered that I should ask my wife for forgiveness, but this time, God made it loud and clear what I needed to do. I said, "Honey I made sexual advancements that day toward something that was not you. Will you forgive me?"

Still emotional, she nodded yes, then something inside me said, "Tell her she is released from the burden." I spoke those words, and a smile spread across her face. She then declared, "I just felt something leave. I am free of something I did not understand."

She admitted, "I knew when you called me in here, something like this was going to happen." Her attitude and actions have not been the same since.

Was this the real reason that I was to start writing? If so, praise Jesus! I am very content to stop here. Until I receive that clarity, we will step back in time and visit the jackass who was still driven by his own selfish desires. This event was quite complicated but so monumental that it had to disrupt the linear flow. Now we will return to the conversations and thought patterns I had after the supernatural visitation of Jesus. Remember what you just read, and that I had thirty more months of training from the Holy Spirit to draw from. As you continue reading, keep that in mind.

CHAPTER 9

—————

THE SUPERNATURAL VISITATION REARRANGED MY understanding of reality. Ten PhD's could try to give me their philosophical explanations for my delusion, but none would have any success. I knew it was true, and no one could convince me otherwise. I did have to do an extensive evaluation of my personal psychological condition.

Three weeks prior to this, I had experienced a near psychotic episode. The hospital gave me heavy doses of OxyContin to manage the pain from the severe burns I had suffered. The withdrawal symptoms I experienced while escaping the clutches of OxyContin were severe. I reduced my pill intake from twelve a day to zero in thirty-six hours. That abrupt stop caused some lingering effects.

My son was the first one I contacted to share this amazing story. My recollection was very clear, since the episode had happened only a few hours earlier. I could tell by my son's response that he was affected almost as much as I was. We talked about all the factors that could cause such a thing to happen, examining any reasonable explanation and trying to understand the meaning of it all.

My son and his wife had been to our house the previous

weekend. My daughter-in-law, a surgical nurse, promptly scolded me for the things I was doing wrong. She examined the large grafted areas and commented how good they looked. The reason I tell you this is to show that they had ample time to experience my mental condition. That was one of the key factors my son focused on: my mental capacity.

"Dad, I have to tell you, had we not been there last weekend to see you, I would have suggested to you a psychotic break," my son told me. "But what I saw last weekend was a mentally recovered, fully intact, cognitively functioning individual."

We quickly dismissed the fact that I had consumed a marijuana brownie. The amount of THC that would have to be ingested to cause a hallucinogenic effect would be tremendous.

As we continued our conversation, he elaborated on the point that I sounded completely in control of my mental faculties. His reasoning led him to believe that something supernatural did in fact happen. Both of us were company CEOs and had had countless opportunities to read individuals. We evaluated what happened in a systematic and controlled way, without jumping to any rash conclusions.

Groups valued my son's input. He was rational and thorough in his reasoning. What we discussed was personal, and I actually asked my son to not even tell his wife about it. That was a mistake and eventually caused some hard feelings. My wife was very protective about what happened and really did not want me to discuss it with anyone. She is a mild-mannered, conservative individual, and she did not dispute the fact that something else was in control. How many people would believe that?

Fortunately, there is much more to the story that will add substantial credibility. I will continue to unravel this self-centered life that was such a mess. You would think that someone who experienced an event such as this would make a 180-degree turn from the direction he was going. The issue of whether or not this was a supernatural visitation from God was settled in my mind. Facts that connected everything were revealed over the next eighteen months.

The next day, I gathered anything related to marijuana and got rid of it. In my mind, it would be impossible to even consider any association with it. The command seemed so direct and forceful that any disobedience could lead to calamity. This was the first time that I realized I may have violated some supernatural contract.

I believe that when God set me free from the bondage of marijuana twenty-three years earlier, a blessing was attached. God was quite pissed off by how far off track I had taken the blessings he had given me. He could not release Himself from His word of a blessing. Just after all this, another significant blessing occurred, at least from my selfish worldly person's perspective.

God had allowed me the gift of being a helicopter and airplane pilot and to own one of each aircraft. After I had stopped drinking and using drugs, I needed something else to obsess over. From my side of the equation, my spiritual life was on life support. Why I did not spend time restoring what I had voluntarily given up was a big mystery. The emptiness that we continually feel inside exists from not having a meaningful relationship with Jesus. My carnal Christian behavior continued to steamroll ahead, even after great revelation. I had not flown in several years, and since my heart attack, I had the additional hurdle of getting back my medical clearance.

A battery of tests and medical evaluations was necessary. I cannot begin to understand how God would continue to give me the desires of my heart. There was probably only a trickle of improvement on my spiritual walk. After being rejected six times for a new medical clearance, I thought I would try one more time. I actually prayed to God and thanked him for all the years I could fly. I told him I would have no hard feelings if I never flew again. That was not just lip service, because I meant it in my heart. One final time, I submitted all the paperwork, and miraculously the element of my heart condition that was preventing me from flying had improved significantly. My cardiologist said there was no explanation for what happened. The FAA has a requirement for the aortic valve, that it be no larger than 4.5 centimeters.

Every previous test put my aortic root at 5.3 to 5.5 centimeters, so there was absolutely no way they were ever going to allow me to fly again. I had surrendered to the idea that I probably would not fly again. I felt God was saying, "Try the seventh time," as though I were dipping in the Jordan River. *2 Kings 5:14 NKJV: "So he went down and dipped seven times in the Jordan, according to the saying of the man of God, and his flesh was restored like the flash of a little child, and he was clean."* I submitted the seventh and final round of paperwork and waited.

Roughly two weeks before I got back the paperwork, I had this distinct feeling that God was telling me I would fly again. We were in the final stages of construction on the new building at my home, but I had not put in the new hangar door yet. I told my wife I was going to go ahead, but she was against the idea, and rightfully so. In my heart, I felt this was an act of faith and that God was testing me, to the point that if I was not obedient to this prompting, I would not get my license back. As unbelievable as it may sound, on my seventh try, I received my medical certificate. Within a short period of time, I bought another helicopter.

The way I viewed it, there was no denying that God permitted great success for me. But four very important words belong at the end of that sentence: "to do His will." That understanding did not arrive in my spirit for several more months. The endless cycle of purchasing one thing after another to fill the emptiness that existed inside me was coming to an end. *Romans 2:8 NKJV: "But to those who are self-seeking and do not obey the truth, but obey unrighteousness indignation and wrath tribulation and anguish on every soul of man who does evil."*

When a person has years of ego and arrogance wrapped around a core of self-indulgence, it is very difficult to penetrate. With the experiences that I had, this process should have been much quicker. My own self-centeredness had blinded me to the reality of God's love.

When we resumed filming *Speed My Ride*, I told the producer, my nephew, we would not be doing the stunts through the building. He was surprised because he had witnessed many of my crazy antics throughout the years. My ego was too big to stop the self-promoting efforts that we had under way. Even though my grafted skin was paper-thin, we resumed filming. The least little rub would cause the new skin to detach. I was so focused on the false belief that I could obtain fame that nothing was going to stand in my way. We had already missed a few weeks of filming due to my accident, so several days a week we recorded footage of various situations.

I am sure that God was thinking, "You have got to be kidding me!" Looking back on this now, I cannot believe he did not send a large lightning bolt to do me in once and for all. In just a few weeks' time, I was bragging to people how quickly I had recovered and that we were continuing to film potential shows. My ego and pride had pushed the great blessing of God's protection out of the equation. I had made the decision that we needed to add four more zip lines on my property, which would end up costing over half a million dollars.

Spending that kind of money would have been ridiculous if I didn't disguise it well. I am not sure if I can put an accurate percentage on it, but I will try. I was getting older, but I still had the ego to want to be the cool guy. In the area where I live, there are not many zipline opportunities. I thought if I could put in some pretty impressive towers and runs, I could draw attention to myself. "Look at me! How great is this?!" My daughter even questioned the reasoning for such a project. God was continually using her to disrupt my thinking. I would have never admitted to such a thing at the time. "It will be a place for youth groups to come and enjoy nature." That was the spin I used on my wife and others. The reality was that more than ninety percent of the true motive was self-centered.

Why was it that certain instructions from the encounter took hold immediately while others were shuffled aside? I was still under the delusion that I was okay. I did enough kind things. I treated people pretty well most of the time. I was generous enough. But there lies the problem. In all of these statements *I* was still the center of my universe. For a week or two, I was deeply humbled by the experience. Amazingly, when arrogance and ego have been chopped, they easily grow back. Not until the root system has been dug out can you actually stop the growth. Now, it was time to get out the backhoe, literally.

We were filming different activities involving the new zip line construction. A backhoe was used to dig the holes for the anchor system. Each hole was roughly twelve feet long and seven feet wide, and five or six feet deep. The anchors that we constructed were three feet wide and eight feet long. We used the Bobcat skid steer to lower them into the holes. The holes were in very wet areas, sometimes filling halfway full or more with water. The installation process went smoothly. The producer said he wanted a little more excitement. Telling this to someone who was full of himself was like giving a dare to the schoolyard bully.

I unloaded the last anchor from the top of our transport vehicle. The cameras were rolling, and I decided to ham it up a bit. I shook the eight-foot anchor as much as I could while I was backing up. Watching only the camera crew, while being unaware of my stupidity, I drove right into the hole, rapidly flipping ninety degrees. Instantly, I realized I was in a tough situation. The Bobcat had bulletproof glass that was nearly an inch thick. The lift was raised right in front of the door. Because of this, the door would barely open. Breaking the glass was not an option, even if I had a sledgehammer. And the hole was halfway full of water that would quickly swallow the Bobcat. I moved myself so that I could try to escape, but the door would open only four or five inches.

My nephew, the producer, was only a few feet away with a terrified look on his face. Once again, something unexplainable happened. I squeezed through the narrow opening almost as if my head and torso were Silly Putty. The words of an egomaniac where the first that came out of my mouth: "Did you get that on film?!" As I looked at the brand-new Bobcat stuffed in a hole, my nephew had a perplexed look on his face. He pointed at the opening and said, "I cannot believe you just got out of there." I turned and looked, and there was barely enough room to stick my hand in the opening.

That instant was the beginning of much deeper realizations. I stood there frozen in time, wondering what else it would take for me to change. A feeling of imminent death descended over my soul. I knew at that moment if I filmed even one more day, it might be my last. Even though I had thoroughly ticked off God, I still continued down my own selfish path. He must have seen a pinprick of hope in a vast wasteland of a human being.

I turned from the Bobcat and looked my nephew straight in the eye and declared, "I am done." Those were the last words I uttered to anyone in the film crew that day. Usually, I was the guy who gave other people a hard time when they did stupid stuff. This was the day I lost the privilege to ever do that again, not that I ever should have done it in the first place. Many weeks later, we got the issues straightened out with the Bobcat, but my issues had a long way to go.

My nephew called the next day and asked when we would start filming again. I answered, "Never. We are done." Of course, he was disappointed. We had spent nearly the entire year filming, editing and preparing. I wasted tons of money on a foolish endeavor. The spirit trapped inside a self-centered shell finally had a crack to work with. The light of God began to break through the darkness in me. *Ephesians 5:8: "You were once in darkness, but now you are light in the Lord. Walk as children of light."* I think I would describe myself at this point as opening my eyes. I was a long way from walking.

There had been many situations in my life where I escaped death. Most of them I would laugh off, saying something like, "No big deal. I guess I am lucky to be alive." I would joke with people about how my guardian angel has to work overtime for me. Sadly, this was most likely the case. Why was it that this particular incident made my life feel finite? Cocky invincibility had been the norm for me for many years. My self-reliance had been a sturdy four-legged chair, but now it had one of the legs kicked out from under it. I still could maintain my lofty position of pride and ego, but I had to be careful which way I leaned.

God is a gracious and loving Creator. I deserved none of what I had. I was not quite at the point of accepting that. I walked around my facility, looking at all the things that were unnecessary. Many of the things that I had viewed as hallmarks of my success where now looking like burdens on my soul. I would let many different people drive some of my exotic cars. This was merely an effort to give some meaning to my selfishness. I reasoned that I was giving an opportunity that most people would not have. The reality was that I was still feeding the monster of "Look at me and my generosity."

I even committed to God that I would use my helicopter to give people free rides. Even in my pursuit of purchasing a helicopter, I was trying to make a deal with God. On my seventh try for my pilot's medical certificate to be reinstated, I made a proposal to God: "If I can fly again, I will give five hundred people rides, if you allow it." Who did I think I was that I could even approach God in such a way? For the first time in my life, I actually tried keeping my word with God. I had this repetitive dream for years. I was flying through the air, talking to people about Jesus. I wasn't in a helicopter; it was just my body flying through the air. It was not until I had given many rides that I realized almost every time I flew someone in my helicopter I spoke about God. Most were not interested in listening, though they would act as though they were for two reasons. One, they were getting a free helicopter ride, and two, they were a captive audience.

In the process of my revealing the hidden motives and thoughts in my life, many things have surfaced. Even the helicopter rides were attempts to be the cool guy. God could see right through my phony persona. He continued to allow me to masquerade as a charitable pilot. Through His grace, I was able to surpass the five hundred rides that I had promised. There was one more pride-filled event when I used the helicopter to showcase how great I was.

For the next several months, I had no real focus. I continued to work on the trails and little projects in my shop. I felt as though something was brewing inside me. A metamorphosis of sorts was preparing me for what the future held. So many ideas were pouring into my mind that it was impossible to digest them all. I was praying more and felt God's presence in new and strong ways. I would have never guessed that God was going to unleash my mind. In doing so, He implanted complex ideas about the human beginning and purpose. The ideas were not straightforward and easy to comprehend. Many times I would walk on the trails and cry out to God. I begged for understanding.

One day in the woods, during one of my pleading sessions, God answered, "Do not worry about the content. Just write down all that I pour into you. These thoughts will be parables of sorts with hidden truths in them. I will use them as a stealth approach. People's attention will be captured in ways they never considered. Your pride and ego will be the only stumbling block. Do not put your name on these books. These are intended for my glory not yours."

No, this was not an audible voice; it was more powerful than that. I could not escape the imprint that it left on my consciousness. If it had been mere audible words, I may have been freed from them, but they were downloaded into the hard drive of my mind.

This was the starting point of something I never dreamed possible. There were many experiences in my life that I would not believe unless I lived them. If someone had told me stories like these, I would have said they were full of it. In this case, a trail of evidence has been strewn along the path like breadcrumbs. That trail is what eventually leads me home, back to the kingdom where I can be a servant to the King. I began the process of taking what was being poured into my mind and pouring it out on paper.

CHAPTER 10

ALL THESE IDEAS COMPILING IN MY MIND NEEDED to be released. I had never written more than a couple paragraphs in forty years. I contacted a few different ghostwriters because I thought, "What do I know about writing a book?" Eventually I identified a successful author and discussed the thoughts that were planted in my mind. He was an arrogant, full-of-himself kind of person. He would go on and on, talking about his accomplishments and success—very similar to the behavior that I demonstrated.

Our first conversation led to the author asking for an outline of what we had discussed. I believe this took place on a Friday. By the following Monday, I had constructed an 11,000-word sentence, which showed just how much assistance I would need. I sent it to him and waited for a response. Something inside me said, "This story needs to come from you." The whole idea of using a ghostwriter felt dishonest. I knew if I were ever asked questions regarding the material, I could not lie.

The day I finished the 11,000-word outline, I started on a second book. God had shaken the bottle of Champagne, and the cork was released with the 11,000 words. Now the geyser erupted in an unstoppable fashion. I became obsessed with getting the words on paper as fast as I could. Had I not been restrained by a human body, it would have happened much quicker. Every day for the next seventy days, I wrote at a feverish pace. My wife and daughter were concerned about my sanity. When I wrote down certain revelations, I got the feeling that the future had just been foretold. I began to question my own mental stability as the stories continued to gush out from me.

I tried to walk in the woods for an hour each day. I would cry out to God and ask him, "What are you doing to me?" I could not understand this unending torrent of ideas. Concepts were revealed to me about life, spirituality, and a far more complex world that exists in the unseen realm. They were fresh ideas that I had never heard before. Abstract thoughts that my finite mind never could have comprehended were now commonplace.

These were not homegrown thoughts that I had concocted in a feeble understanding of life. They were supernaturally implanted for a purpose. I know I am not to concern myself with what that purpose is. Countless times, I felt God warning me, "Your pride is the biggest hurdle you have. This book shall never bear your name. The only way this will get screwed up will be because of yourself." The reason I feel as though I need to emphasize this point is because I nearly did screw it up.

Exactly three weeks after the initial call with the ghostwriter, book number one was completed. Seventy-five thousand words had made their way into this reality. When we talked, the ghostwriter could not believe how that was even possible. That made two of us. When I read back through the words I had written, it was if I were reading them for the first time. I found myself in a small bubble on the story timeline. During the process of writing, I could recall a short distance back in the story and a short distance forward. That was the only place that my focus was allowed to be.

I went on to write the next 75,000-word book in another twenty-one days. By the time I had a conversation with the ghost writer about the first 75,000-word book, I had completed the next one. He had postponed reading any of the material because, in his mind, it was probably near worthless. After he did read some, his position drastically changed. He had skill and craft of sentence structure, punctuation, story flow and more that I did not have. That was not what I was called to do. The task that was laid before me was to convey the thoughts that were being implanted in my mind. The fact that I was an engineer-inventor type helped my description make at least some basic sense. I was only the mouthpiece, and God was the instrument that made the music. Without His inspiration, not one sound would have been heard. *1 Corinthians 15:58 NKJV: "Therefore, my beloved brethren, be steadfast, immovable, always abounding in the work of the Lord, knowing that your labor is not in vain in the Lord."*

The communication with the ghostwriter continued. At this point, it became more of a collaborative effort. His ability to add details to the characters and scenes was light years beyond mine. Actually, I did not have abilities in this area and did not feel that I should even concern myself with the descriptions. God knew that my pride was still an issue I had not yet dealt with. He also knew it was a big risk even to put somebody such as myself in this position. I would have doubted God's wisdom in this for quite some time. The more comments that I received from other individuals concerning the stories, the more my ego wanted to take ownership for what was occurring. There was a handful of people who I enlisted to feed my ego with positive feedback. During the writing process, I would share entire stories.

Only by reflection did I see part of God's purpose. I had not traveled down the path of surrender far enough yet to see it. One of the primary elements of the storyline was how to become selfless. God was not only talking through me; he was talking to me. A large portion of one of the books dealt with connecting mentally with other humans during their life experiences. The purpose was to gain empathy and understanding. During my times of writing, I would feel the sense of those realities, almost as I described it happening. Had I pondered what God was trying to teach me more deeply, revelation would have occurred sooner. These thoughts and feelings would linger only briefly. The desire to continually fuel my ego always pulled rank over everything else.

Initially, it was somewhat innocent, but it quickly grew into a habit that needed constant replenishing. Now I had found a different avenue to feed the look-at-me monster. The need to get this fix on a regular basis was just as potent as any heroin addiction. I started to convey to my wife and daughter comments that individuals were making about my writing. Both of them had adverse reactions to what I was doing. They clearly detected in me what God hated. Pride had simply discovered a new avenue to exploit my fallen nature.

I still had all the fancy cars, and a new helicopter. I was proud of the very expensive renovation and expansion. Now the removal of spotlight filming of myself was replaced with spotlight writing of myself. The idea that God implanted in me to "Keep yourself out of this" became more of a "Yeah, yeah, sure. God forgives me." The pure arrogance and disrespect of such a thought troubles my spirit, but this is the truth of the situation. The instant we have these kinds of thoughts, we should immediately repent and reposition ourselves properly before the Creator.

Left unchecked, ego is like a truck that is going down a mountainside and has lost its brakes. The speed and momentum continue to increase, leading to an inevitable crash. The ghostwriter comparing my storytelling abilities to famous authors was like throwing gasoline on a fire. The accelerant effect on my ego was instantaneous.

For the first time in my life, God had successfully shown me enough of myself for me to start considering my ways. If I would have heeded His warnings, I could have avoided many more lessons that were now needed. The small gains that God had shown me in my spiritual understanding were quickly swept away.

As ridiculous as this sounds, my mind was already leaping to movie deals and world fame brought on by these "amazing books." The continued resistance from my wife and daughter acted as a point of division in our family. They could see the situation the way it really was, while I was blind. If only I had followed the instructions that God gave me, I would have been much closer with God, much sooner. *1 Timothy 6:20 NKJV: "Guard what was committed to your trust, avoiding the profane and idle babblings and contradictions of what is falsely called knowledge, by professing it some have strayed concerning the faith."*

All I needed to do was value what God entrusted to me. It was as if I had found a book lying in the field and crossed off the author's name and wrote mine in its place. After all, these ideas for the books formed much faster than my human mind was capable of. In my household, talking about the books or anything pertaining to them was completely discontinued, but not because of my obedience to God. I made this decision to protect my precious ego. I did not need my daughter or wife trying to put me in my place. I was such a foolish man.

I was listening to Christian rock music at this time, particularly a Christian hip-hop rock 'n' roll band out of New Zealand. They had moved to Nashville to pursue success in America. I felt as though their music somehow seeped into the pages of the books I was writing. Through all my prideful selfishness, I was still able to sense the prompting of God. I had the crazy idea of collaborating with this band. Through the band's manager, I was able to set up a meeting with the lead singer, Brad. We met in Nashville and spent three hours together. I was considerably older than he was, old enough to be his father.

For some reason, we really hit it off. He asked me to send him a copy of the first book. All I had was my first draft available for him to read. Before leaving the meeting, I told him, "It does not matter what you think, because if God wants you to be involved, you will be." A few days later, he called me and wanted to read book two. He said when he read the books, music would play in his head. His next words were, "Dude, I am in." Brad's band ended up producing five songs and a trailer of the highest quality for the book.

The interactions and communication with Brad were quite good. During these times, God showed me that everything does not have to be about me. I genuinely wanted to see how our collaboration could benefit Brad, maybe even more so than myself. I was most comfortable driving in my own personal lane of selfishness, but God had been putting more and more obstacles in front of me, causing me to veer out of my lane. I was seemingly incapable of not eventually going back to that prideful, selfish, ego-driven road hog side of my life.

My life continued on, and it happened to be the year of my fortieth class reunion. How convenient for me to have an entertainment venue with zip lines and walking trails all packaged in a pride-filled present with an ego bow on top. I met with the reunion planners and humbly (yeah, right) offered my facility at no charge. I even came up with a plan to have donations to a local food bank contributed for classmates who had died.

This was an egomaniac's dream come true. All my former classmates could see how successful I was. They could even take pictures of the cars and motorcycles I had. On top of that, I would be gracious enough to offer free helicopter rides. When someone's motives start out wrong, no matter what they do to dress up the situation, it does not change the starting point. The fact is, I wanted attention and admiration from my peers. If only I had spent my efforts pursuing praise and glory for the Creator of the universe, there would have been meaning.

Imagine a wretched pile of manure. You can cover it with as many good acts as you want. You can throw diamonds and rubies on it until it is completely covered. Then you can douse it with gallons of perfume. You come back the next day, and what do you have? A huge, stinking pile of manure. That is the reality of most of the things that I did as a carnal Christian. If you do not let the Holy Spirit reveal the pile and help you shovel it out, you will always be a stinking pile of manure.

This continual trap of behavior had a simple solution: full and complete surrender to Jesus Christ, without any loopholes, sidebars or contingency plans. I had allowed myself to be in a self-induced torture chamber because I was unwilling to let someone else call the shots. *Proverbs 26:11–12: "As a dog returns to his own vomit, so a fool repeats his folly. Do you see a man wise in his own eyes? There is more hope for a fool than for him."*

Little by little, God was trying to nudge me forward on my spiritual path, but first, I needed to release my lifetime of worldly baggage. Would I ever be able to soar on wings of eagles? No, not if I kept getting in the way. God had a few more things up His robe, but they were just the right things to add into the mix of incredible situations that I had already encountered. I am continuously amazed by His long-suffering and patience with me. I still am, and always will be, a work in progress. My prayer is that this example of a life lived horribly, but still redeemed by God, will give hope to anyone.

CHAPTER 11

————

MY MOTHER WAS A SELFLESS PERSON. SHE DEMON-strated what Jesus instructed and showed no fanfare, self-promotion, or attention-seeking personal motives whatsoever. Her loving kindness was always a beacon that drew people closer to what a person should be. She had this uncanny ability to make everyone who she interacted with feel like her favorite. I believe she directly got this characteristic from Jesus Himself. Everyone who came in contact with her had a sense of the extraordinary person she was. My son com-mented that "Grandma did not have much from a worldly standpoint, but she was the richest woman I knew."

I do not have a full understanding of what the Authority of God was referring to concerning my mother. The fact that there were only a few like her was made quite clear. She viewed her humility and kindness as ordinary and common. She thought nothing of it and believed that was expected of all of us. When I would highlight certain attributes of her behavior, she would just brush it off. Then she would say, "Everyone is like that." She was aware that some people act poorly, but generally she thought her behavior was just "normal."

I told her she would have a hard time walking around in heaven. She always gave me a troubled look when I said this. Then I would complete my thought by telling her that her crown in heaven will be so heavy she will have trouble holding it up. She would dismiss what I said and then say, "I will just be glad to be there." *1 Peter 5:2–4 NKJV: "Shepherd the flock of God which is among you, serving as overseers, not by compulsion but willingly, not for dishonest gain but eagerly, nor as being lords over those entrusted to you, but being examples to the flock, and when the chief Shepherd appears, you will receive the crown of glory that does not fade away."*

Many of my mother's characteristics were ingrained in her being. For her, it was not a matter of learning and becoming a better person. Instead, she just lived out the truth that was in her. After all, anyone who could raise eight children and have twenty-six foster children had to be special.

I could easily fill a book highlighting her many humble acts of obedience. The dichotomy that existed in me troubled her, I am sure. Most likely, the many prayers that she offered on my behalf had a greater influence than I realized. My father and mother lived a simple life—a stark contrast to the path that I chose. I want to highlight a few aspects about her to demonstrate the great example she was. Had I emulated even a small part of her character, the roots of pride would not have grown so deep. Care and compassion for my immediate family were never an issue. That is a very closed-minded worldly view of what love is. The reality of humanity is that it gravitates toward that model. On the other hand, my mother modeled a different approach. *Mark 12:31 NKJV: "And the second, like it is this, you shall love your neighbor as yourself. There is no other commandment greater than these."*

My mother spent the final two and a half years of her life in a nursing home. She had Alzheimer's/dementia. The dreaded day came when she did not recognize us anymore. The amazing thing about her life was that it transcended her mental faculties. Everyone who came in contact with her commented about how special she was, even when her verbal skills and cognitive ability had faded. The presence of Jesus living in her was so strong that it would affect people on a level they could not understand. Most of the nursing home staff said she was their favorite. I would estimate that more than ninety percent of the days that she spent in the nursing home she had a visitor. That in itself is a testament to the love she had poured out all those years.

As her remaining weeks and days were winding down, I considered the power of her life in much greater detail. Why was I not more like her? Was there any way to be more like her? Was it even possible for somebody at my age to really change? Many times when I went to see her I was not focused on her. I would be thinking about going out to eat afterward or picking up something at the store. I am sure a number of other things also cluttered my mental focus on my dear mother.

Many times, I would leave and go to our vehicle, thinking my wife was right behind me. We would exchange the appropriate sign or nod, indicating we were going to go. My wife would linger several minutes, sometimes longer. Quite frequently, I was not very patient. This is a sad fact to reflect on, that my wife was showing more love to my mother then I was. One of the most endearing things about my wife was how much she loved my mother. That is an undeniable indicator of the selfishness that still existed in me. She would always explain upon her return how hard it was to leave my mother's side. I am sure there were times that I would say, "What difference does it make? She is not going to remember anyway." I shed tears admitting to this, because I realize what a selfish a-hole I was.

The Holy Spirit is reminding me of other behaviors that I must confess. Because my mother's memory was failing, we thought a whiteboard could be helpful for writing reminders, so my wife and I picked up a couple small ones and hung them on a wall in her room. The staff noted that within a few minutes of our leaving, my mother would forget that we had even been there. We decided to use one board as a monthly calendar and the other as a message board. The calendar board became a method of recording family members' visits. This would enable the staff to say so-and-so was just here.

Most likely I was the only family member who counted the number of days each of us visited Mother. I rarely considered the amount of time or quality of time. "I would ask why some person or another was not spending more time with her while I was boasting about my three-days-a-week record. The mind of a self-centered, egotistical individual will use whatever situation is at hand to propagate their own illusions. This behavior, upon reflection, seems so petty and useless. I should have used the same energy to focus on my lovely mother. I will never know how much richer and more meaningful the conversations could have been.

The other whiteboard became a showcase for my poetry-writing skills. If I had access to a large-screen TV in the commons area, I probably would have displayed my poems there. I am sure that I thought I was far more clever than I actually was. Many times, I wondered why no one would comment on my Shakespeare-level work. My wife and I would get an occasional chuckle out of the poems. On rare occasions, I actually put heartfelt effort into the writing, while thinking of my mother. But other motives always negated that sincerity. Lurking in my selfish mind somewhere was an ego monster wanting to be fed.

To document my (not) excellent work, I would take pictures of the poems with my phone. I could use the photos someday to compile a book and show how thoughtful and considerate of a son I was. Whoops, I mean how wonderful and kind my mother was. See how easy it is to get things twisted around. We can disguise our motives in the most precious and dear ways. *Philippians 2:3 NKJV: "Let nothing be done through selfish ambition or conceit, but in lowliness of mind let each esteem others better than himself."* I know what the verse says, but it really was not written for me, because my mother knew I was sincere (yeah, right.) Countless times, I actually thought this behavior was okay. I was only fooling myself, because I certainly was not fooling God.

The unfortunate part of this reality is that I was a troublesome kid to raise. If anyone needed to demonstrate a contrite heart in his behavior, it was me. I thought that I sincerely loved my parents, but I chose to demonstrate that love in a pattern I was familiar with. I tried to offset the afflictions that I had caused with my behavior by buying things for my parents. I think it affected me more than it did them. I equated forgiveness, remorse and accountability with a dollar amount. Once a particular dollar amount had been reached, surely they would forgive or overlook all my transgressions.

There was an element of "Look at me. I can afford to buy this for them." I would have never admitted that at the time, however, any justification at this point demonstrates lack of transparency. If you believe you are transparent, I challenge you to pray to God to reveal yourself, to yourself, through your own words. Are you obedient to the power of the Holy Spirit inside you? The written word will reveal more truth than the words you speak. Our tongue has learned to be deceitful in the most miniscule ways. Maybe it is because our eyes are a window to the soul. For me, there seems to be a stronger connection when I see the words. Any degree of deception makes me uneasy in my spirit, which in turn makes me correct the words until the uneasiness departs. The fallen nature of our flesh is probably what allows our tongues to be so deceitful.

The final twenty-four hours of my mother's life was an agonizing experience. Anyone who has seen someone go through the labored breathing of the final few hours knows exactly what I am talking about. Thankfully, hospice had her heavily sedated, and I believe for the most part she was unaware. I prayed more than I had ever prayed before. "Please Lord, do not let her suffer. Take her peacefully. Make that labored breathing stop. Please Lord, give her Your everlasting peace."

Her body would arch up off the bed with each breath; her lungs were no longer capable of drawing in sufficient breath on their own. The strong will that had made her such an admirable woman was now fighting for her life. Her will was never used for personal gain, but always for the benefit of others. Her struggle for life continued. Each muscle contraction would cause the lungs to eke out a bit more air. I talked with some of my brothers outside her room and made an alarming proposal.

Because I was such a know-it-all, it is not surprising what I suggested. I actually proposed covering her mouth with my hand to end her life. At that moment, I would have followed through. I would say that it was a fifty-fifty proposition for me. Half of me desperately wanted to put my mother out of her misery. The other half could hardly listen to another gasp for air. On the surface, this could be viewed as an honorable thing to do, but there is a huge flaw in that thinking. I was not her creator. What right did I have to end her life? Thankfully, this was one very stupid thing that I did not do. My brothers shared my anxiety, but based on their response, I knew they would not support the action. Late in the evening, we decided to take shifts with our mother. My sister stayed at her side, and a few hours later, my mother went to be with the Lord.

My sister had a very difficult time when my father died. Because of that, she needed to be at our mother's side at the end. I must tell you a few more things about my mother. There was a reason that the Authority of God made a specific declaration concerning her. There was an innocence that God shielded inside of her. For whatever reason, certain things of this world were never able to penetrate it. I am not insinuating that she was anything beyond human, or infallible to the temptations of the flesh, but her actions indicated a close walk with God. I would not have been surprised if she just disappeared like Enoch did. *Hebrews 11:5 NKJV: "By faith Enoch was taken away so that he did not see death, and was not found, because God had taken him, for before he was taken he had this testimony, that he pleased God."*

My mother had many traits that showed Jesus was living in her. Her willingness to accept outsiders into her life and home seemed endless. The sheer number of children who passed through the old farmhouse doors was amazing. Many of these children stayed in contact with her long after they entered adulthood. The horrendous living conditions that some of these children had suffered caused them mental stability issues, but that did not matter to my mother; she just loved them more. I could never understand why she would purposely put herself in difficult situations. The concept of unconditional love never registered with me.

When someone threw tantrums or had violent outbursts, she would cradle the offender in her arms. Many times, she would have them sit on her lap, and together they would rock back and forth in the old rocking chair. The soothing rhythm and a loving embrace did wonders to bring stability back to the situation. Many times I benefited from that loving care. For whatever reason, the compassion and empathy that came so naturally to her did not take hold in me. You would think that at least by osmosis I would have absorbed some of her virtue. This was only a small example of my mother's love.

The umbrella of her love was large and did not seem to preclude anybody. She cared for both of her aunts and their husbands in their older years. When her father died in his fifties, she moved her mother into our house. Eventually, she and my father built an apartment connected to their house where my grandmother lived most of the remainder of her life. When my grandmother asked to be put in a retirement home due to increasing care needs, my mother was very resistant. Not long after my grandmother moved out, a neighbor moved into the apartment. My mother had an addiction, and it never could be satisfied. She was always looking for her next fix. The only way to satisfy her desire was to find somebody else to love. That is probably the only God-approved addiction.

My behavior in grade school was less than stellar. An older principal, Miss Price, was in charge of the school. I do not believe that my mother ever got a call concerning her other children. If there was a speed dial back then, I am sure Miss Price would have had our home phone number on it. That's how frequently I ended up in the principal's office. My tendency to be deceitful to cover up my behavior made trusting anything I said nearly impossible. But there was one particular incident in which I was innocent.

Miss Price had called my mother to the school once again. Something had occurred in one of the classrooms, and I happened to be present. It was assumed that in some way I was involved. I was dismissed from school for the rest of the day and went home with my mother. Pleading with her, I explained the situation. I told her there was a corroborating witness who happened to be a neighbor. A few days later, my mother received confirmation that my explanation was true. She felt it was necessary to bring it to the principal's attention. Miss Price refused to accept the new information and firmly believed that I was just a bad apple.

This was very upsetting to my mother. She even cried at home for me. She felt it was a great injustice to be sentenced erroneously without full consideration of the facts, even though my sentencing was only expulsion for half a day. A sense of fairness and justice ran deep within her. This understanding is necessary before I reveal the rest of the story. Miss Price had never married and had no family. She lived in the same home with her father and took care of him until his death. Eventually, she retired from the school and became old and feeble. Who do you think took care of her?

Miss Price had saved her money and accumulated quite a bit. My family was poor, but my mother would take meals to Miss Price several times a week. She never received any compensation. My father often would question why she was doing it. "She could easily afford to have a paid staff take care of her," my father would say. My mother's response was, "She is all alone, and she needs someone to love her."

I can remember one time that my mother came home from a visit quite excited.

Apparently, Miss Price had a collection of knickknacks, plates, saucers, cups and various other items. The collection includes some very nice pieces. Miss Price had given my mother an old, chipped cup, yet you would have thought she just received a million dollars. My father was astounded by the joy my mother demonstrated for that "old piece of crap cup." To my mother, the object was unimportant. She valued it because it showed that someone thought she was worthy of receiving a gift. Try giving your kids a chipped cup for

Christmas and see how that flies. This is a woman who lived the true meaning of a servant heart. *Ephesians 4:32 NKJV: "Be kind to one another, tenderhearted, forgiving one another, even as God in Christ forgave you."*

My mother could have easily reasoned why Miss Price did not deserve any special care. Those reasons that trip so many of us up were never trigger points for her. Remember, this was a woman who had plenty of money to pay someone for care. This was a woman who was not particularly kind or lovable. This was a woman who refused to recant a false accusation against a troubled boy. This was a woman who made no close friends her entire life. This was a woman for whom my parents really could not afford to provide food. This was a woman who took our mother's time for her own personal care. This was a woman who showed little gratitude for the love she was shown. I am in awe that I had a mother who was able to see beyond all of the stumbling blocks.

Reflecting back on my mother's life made me realize what an awesome example she was. Many times, I would joke with my siblings that our mother set the bar too high. None of us would ever be able to obtain what she did so naturally. In our own strength, that is an accurate statement. With Christ, all things are possible. The prayer "Please Lord, show me how to be more like my mother" ran on a loop in my mind. In the months that followed my mother's death, I would pray, "Please Lord, show me how to become more like you." As God opened up my understanding, He revealed to me that all of the exceptional qualities my mother had were because of Jesus shining through her. The way God answered my prayer was unconventional. The process of chipping away at my pride and ego had really just begun, and there were literally thousands of miles more to travel down that path.

CHAPTER 12

———

AFTER MY MOTHER'S PASSING, A SENSE OF EMPTINESS surrounded me. I still did not feel as though my wife or daughter was supporting my efforts as an author or my other endeavors. I had become so accustomed to having a self-focused spotlight that I felt abandoned if it were not on. I reasoned that everything I was doing was good and pleasing to God. Many of my troubling behaviors were now gone. I had established a nonprofit to help promote selflessness. We were constructing an adventure park of sorts on our property. I would even comment on how proud of me my parents would be since some of their original farm property was going to be used for the park—just another feeble attempt to cover up my ego-driven actions.

My wife and daughter had an uncanny ability to X-ray right to the heart. No matter what kind of dress I put on the pig, it was still a pig, and they knew it. Since my reasoning and my will were still in the driver's seat of my life, I was blinded to the truth. Daily life in my household became contentious. I felt like I was on an island, isolated from my family, and I was the only one who could see all the good things I was trying to do.

God was trying to reveal the true nature of my heart. Satan was trying to keep me blind to the fact that I was useless as a servant to the King. Do not think for one second that if you demonstrate any of the behaviors I did that God will approve of your actions. All of us need to make improvements, and here is a big indicator why it is true. *Think about this to the count of five.* When I say you need to make improvements, in your heart, how do you respond? "He does not know me, so how can he make such accusations?" "I am just fine the way I am." If those, or a variation of those, are your answers, you're guilty. This is why: If you did not ask the Holy Spirit to take a personal inventory, you are responding in the flesh. I am assuming that you have surrendered to the Lordship of Jesus Christ and are on the journey of obedience to the Bible. I hope and pray that is the case, and if so, the Holy Spirit will point out unnecessary baggage.

I am getting a bit ahead of myself because my personal timeline had not been awakened to that point yet. Due to my wife's apparent inability to recognize all the "goodness" within me, I became resentful. I figured maybe it would be better without her, and I was just sick and tired of the last two years without support. After all, I had provided a lavish lifestyle for her, and she had not worked in nearly a quarter of a century. Justification of one's own actions are easy when you have the kind of mindset I had.

Roughly a week before I undertook my first twenty-one-day excursion, things were unsettled between my wife and me. Actually, I had considered just disappearing. I went online and searched for ways to become untraceable. I also searched out locations, religious organizations, Christian cult groups—anywhere or any way that I could fade into another existence. There was no question that some deep, unknown battle was raging in my soul. My thoughts would jump from one extreme to another as fast as a coin could flip heads or tails. Some of my thoughts would push me toward the goodness of God. Others showed me how much misery I could cause my wife if I left her forever.

There was a break in the stormy waters of my soul: My wife and I were able to have in-depth, calm communication with each other. After nearly three decades of marriage, this was the first time we reached such a level of conversation. Prior to these discussions, I had mentioned the idea of going on a spiritual journey of discovery. After a few days of sincere and open communication, I believe my wife viewed that as an empty threat. Many times, I would say hurtful and mean things just to cause harm. This time, it was not just hot air, because a few days later my words came to fruition. I allowed something that she said to me bruise my malnourished ego. This quickly led to a selfish gust that took over my soul. "Fine," I said, "I will show you." Just like that, I began a three-thousand-mile road trip.

For the first few days, I did not tell her where I was going. I ended up in Sarasota, Florida. I know, it already sounds suspicious to leave the twenty-degrees weather of Michigan for eighty-degrees Florida. I can say with nearly complete honesty, the weather was not much of a consideration. I had investigated several states as possible destinations. They were scattered around the country, in various temperature zones. The location where I ended up was exactly where I was supposed to be. The fifty-year-old hotel right on the ocean was reasonably priced and starkly different from the modern high-rises a few miles away.

At this point in my life, I had eliminated drinking, smoking, doing drugs or going to topless bars. Just so the record is straight, I have not visited a topless bar for many, many years, but there is a reason why I am mentioning it. Billboards advertising most of the vices that I had engaged in during my life were prevalent, or my awareness of them was heightened. There was a high probability that Satan was stirring thoughts in my mind to derail God's plan.

When I entered the state of Florida, I saw many billboards showing pole dancers. Satan was whispering in my ear, "Nobody will know. You are more than a thousand miles from home, and you deserve it. Look at how your wife was treating you. It is not like you are going to be sleeping with them. What is it really going to hurt?" These thoughts were setting a trap in my mind that would later be sprung by fleshly desire. If I would have had more of God's Word in my heart, I would have been prepared. *1 Corinthians 10:13 NKJV. "No temptation has overtaken you accept such as is common to man, but God is faithful, who will not allow you to be tempted beyond what you are able, but with the temptation will also make the way of escape, that you may be able to bear it."*

This Bible verse has been buried in my mind for decades. I had called on it to successfully overcome temptation many times. The fact that I have piled layers upon layers of crap on top of it made it nearly impossible to retrieve. Had I deemed it important enough to be floating on the surface of my awareness, sin could have been prevented. I settled into my apartment and started to construct a story. I boastfully claimed that God sent me on this journey and I was to do twelve acts of kindness/charity to represent the twelve days of Christmas. An ego-driven person always has an angle. For whatever reason, God allowed me to believe the illusion my mind had fabricated, but then He used it for his own purpose.

In my efforts to make my story seem believable, I contacted several charities. The Salvation Army, a local rescue mission, a hospice, and a few others. I was sure that God was behind all of this. Without reaching the point of complete surrender, I could do no better than this. I decided to chronicle my daily experiences in a journal. There was no specific reason, except maybe the entries could become famous memoirs from a brilliant author. Yuck. The reality of one's self is hard to accept when revealed by the light of Jesus.

On a daily basis, I forwarded my journal entries to my wife. This did not start until four or five days after I had arrived in Florida. Almost immediately, she assumed I was on a nice vacation, writing another book. Initially, those thoughts were not above the fold. I did not want to incur the criticisms of the past, especially since she had rejected all of my previous work. My attitude and actions certainly solidified her opinion. There was a reason God made it extremely clear my name was not to be on the books. My wife was far more astute about recognizing the extreme pride that possessed me.

Sharing my journal entries with my wife was a semi-honest attempt to share my daily experiences with her. Most of it was true, except for the parts about how God had ordained so much of it. I, not God, made certain embellishments. Reading back through those entries, I see that the Holy Spirit has revealed more of my deceitful nature. Here is another test for those who believe they are fully committed. *Record yourself doing a sincere verbal confession, then write it out word-for-word and see if the Holy Spirit checks you on it.* If you think you are "all set," then you are not. But if the Holy Spirit does not question your honesty, then you are probably on the right path.

There is something powerful about viewing the words, because they do not disappear like sound waves. Once spoken words have escaped our vocal cords and passed beyond anyone who could hear them, there is no record. We may deceive ourselves into thinking that is true, but God hears us. *Matthew 12:36-37 NKJV: "I say to you that for every idle word men may speak, they will give account of it in the day of judgment. For by your words you will be justified, and by your words you will be condemned."* Jesus makes it quite clear there is no room for debate.

As I read through my journal entries, I realized how flashy they really were. God continues to open up my understanding. My old ways become ridiculous when evaluated by the light of the Holy Spirit. I made this journey with blinders on. The blockages were self-imposed, and I am sure they caused me to miss many things that God put into play. One of the many great attributes about God is He can put a situation in front of you that you cannot get around. One way or another, you will deal with it. Remember the prayer I had, to be more like Jesus. God put scenarios right in front of me.

I will take a few words to reiterate my inability to learn from my surroundings. My mother was a constant example of Christ-like behavior. Compassion, empathy, sincere concern and love were her mainstays. I did not display these characteristics to anyone beyond my immediate family. God influenced me to write three books. One of the primary objectives was to turn away from selfishness and become selfless. Nevertheless, I continued uninhibited on my journey of pride and ego, even after finishing the books. Repeatedly, I had prayed to be more like my mother. In reality, it was to be more like Jesus, but I was not fully aware of that fact at the time. No wonder the Authority of God was irritated by my flippant behavior.

Now it is round three, and God is going to take the gloves off, but so is Satan. He knows that God is awakening something within me that has been dormant for very long. A large portion of one of the books deals with riding along with someone else's awareness to experience their thoughts and emotions. This all takes place in a supernatural realm for the spirits to understand humans and empathy. I am not claiming any substantiated facts in this, but instead a parable of sorts. The greater their understanding becomes, the higher their potential to be agents of change are. You can disregard as trash everything I have said in this book so far if you feel so inclined. But what I will share next will likely snag your attention.

The twelve days of Christmas and twelve acts of kindness are a bunch of bunk advocated by me. This fallacy is what God used to get me in a situation for Him to work. On the seventh morning of my journey, I was listening to the news and learned that it was the six-month anniversary of the killing of forty-nine people at the Pulse nightclub in Orlando. Remember my using the analogy of God hitting me over the head with a two-by-four? This was one of those moments. God made it quite clear in my mind that I was to drive to Orlando that day. Of course, I began to run down the reasons why that was not going to work into my schedule.

I felt it was too far, but God pressed me to simply google it. "Oh, that is a bummer, only ninety miles away. God, I am probably not the best person for the job." I am not homophobic, and I just could not understand why I was supposed to go there. What I needed was God's help, and He would not let me off the hook. Certainly the impression in my mind left no room for disobedience. Since my uptake was rather slow, God now created a scenario for me to live out what I had written about in the book. He was going to show me how to have empathy, compassion and love for all humanity. He was going to start with one of the groups who did not receive enough of those sentiments from others. I got in my truck and began the ninety-mile ride.

I had spent the previous afternoon and evening in a very wealthy vacation community. This was the first time I had ever seen so many high-priced cars clustered in one area. That morning, there was a car show that featured at least fifty Porsches. There were Mercedes, Lexus, and Audi cars, and a few Ferraris sprinkled in. While driving and gawking at the cars, I nearly ran into a couple crossing the road. That evening, I walked around the community asking a question, "What advice would you give about how to live life?" I interviewed forty-two people, and you can imagine the self-serving, arrogant comments that I received. Only two people out of the entire group mentioned God. That there were only two was disappointing, but both seemed genuine about the proclamation.

This was my miniscule attempt to learn about compassion and empathy. Now it was time for God to take over and adjust my approach. *Isaiah 55:8-9 NKJV: "For my thoughts are not your thoughts, nor are your ways my ways, says the Lord. For as the heavens are higher than the earth, so are my ways higher than your ways, and my thoughts than your thoughts."* His ways are definitely far beyond my ways. On my drive to Orlando, God revealed just how far ahead He was. My daily journaling was extensive. I would even write about people I met on my morning walk, and the names of their dogs, so it is astonishing that there is no record of the three additional questions I would be posing to people I met. When I arrived at the Pulse nightclub with my little notebook in hand, I started recording the answers to the four questions.

Thinking back on these questions put me in the minds of other people as much as humanly possible. The order of these questions seemed to put people at ease, and unbelievably more than ninety-eight percent of the people I asked answered them. I still managed to screw up what God was trying to achieve. The many layers of pride went right to my very core. Like an onion has layers, I had many barriers, and there was a strong, unpleasant odor to them. The odor was the realization of the true piece of crap I really was, but for the first time in my life, my understanding was changing.

The questions were: 1) What advice would you give about how to live life? 2) What is the best thing that ever happened to you? 3) What is the worst thing that ever happened to you? 4) How can humanity love one another better? These questions drilled down to the essence of the person. You would think that people would reject a total stranger coming up to them and asking these questions. Maybe it was God's interaction that caused so many to participate. Maybe the real subject in this questioning was me. Could it be that I was the one who had to gain knowledge, not the people who answered the questions?

The answers I received were revealing. Interacting with the LGBTQ crowd at such a solemn event began to change me. The answers were also somewhat similar. I attribute that largely to the event we were attending. I would have never dreamed of attending such an event, let alone interviewing people. This seventh day of my journey was now taking on deeper meanings. To this day, it is still a mystery how the other three questions came about. If you believe in the supernatural power of God, then it is quite simple.

After I had interviewed twenty people at the nightclub, the perimeter gates were opened. These gates had surrounded the complex ever since the massacre. Walking onto the grounds where so many died made people appear as though they were struggling through a pool of molasses. There was a larger black woman who had traveled all the way from California to attend the event. She was distraught and trembling. We made eye contact, and she came and stood next to me. She asked if she could hold my hand, and I gladly accepted. This was the first real indicator that something was going on inside me that was unexpected.

Police helicopters hovered above, and police cars and officers were everywhere. Explaining the sensations that I felt there is difficult: surreal, eerie and troubled, yet I also felt unity and love. Finally, empathy and compassion had begun the slow IV drip into my soul. God had finally discovered a way to minister soul-saving medicine. My soul, which had been largely deprived of empathy and compassion for others, now felt the effects of God's love. Many more drips were needed to see a noticeable change, but the process had started.

God knew this was a point of decision for me. Could the icy grips of pride and ego be successfully removed? Would I continue to make the steps in the right direction, or would I spin back into the orbit that I found so comfortable for many years? God was not the only one who noticed something changing. Satan became aware that I was no longer giving into his ways so easily. Most everyone is caught up in the plethora of entertainment choices or the acquisition of worldly riches, neither of which will stand the test of the eternal fire. God regards all such things as useless. I want to make sure everyone understands this clearly. The obedience I refer to is being completely sold out to the world. If you think you can be playing for both teams, you are wrong. *Matthew 6:24 NKJV: "No one can serve two masters, for either he will hate the one and love the other, or else he will be loyal to the one and despise the other. You cannot serve God and money."*

Let me set the scenario for you a bit further. How about NFL football for a game of choice? There are eleven players per side and four fifteen-minute quarters. Have you ever seen a player go to the other team and play for even one second? How do you think you can dedicate outlandish amounts of time to personal entertainment? There are many categories to choose from. Satan has done a great job of offering a smorgasbord of distractions. The reason I am so hardcore on the subject is because I was a chief offender. Trust me, you cannot serve two masters. If there is anything in your life that keeps you from spending time with God or in His Word, you need to take a hard look at it, then ask yourself why.

CHAPTER 13

TO GIVE A QUANTITATIVE DESCRIPTION OF HOW much Satan tempted me versus the desires of my flesh is difficult. The dichotomy of the two forces battling for control of my soul was real. Most of my life, even though I called myself a Christian, I never posed any significant threat to the kingdom of darkness. Whether I would admit it or not, I was already in his camp. This was not a spy mission either; it was to partake in what the prince of darkness offered his troops: the world and everything in it.

The plan of God to expose me directly and personally through people was evident. This caused the enemy to release attacks against me on a couple different fronts. I was not nearly grounded enough in Scripture and understanding of God to put up much of a defense. Since I was ill equipped to stand up against the fiery darts, I started taking some direct hits. Once again, I have to confess some dark realities about my behavior. My wife was growing increasingly concerned about our relationship. By her own acknowledgment, she had allowed herself to have conversations with people who were more disruptive than supportive. What had begun as an innocent spiritual journey had become an abandonment of my wife and daughter. Instead of trying to bring her out of the misconceptions, I fueled the fire.

Our communication skills were inept. This was primarily because of my dominant behavior, which I had perfected over the years. People urged her to stand up to me, so I would resort to verbal bullying to try to maintain control. With her newfound resolve, combined with my hard-headed self-righteousness, things disintegrated quickly. The toilet was flushed, and the negative comments swirled around the bowl until things descended into the cesspool of unloving behavior. By far, I was the one who added more crap to this equation.

My desire for sexual interaction has always been strong. For the many years I was working ninety- to one-hundred-hour weeks, it was curtailed substantially. Now that I had been home without the burden of long hours, things changed. I frequently enjoyed personal time with my wife. She even said that it seemed more intimate than when we were first married. I am giving these details only so you can have some framework to reference the darker side of what I am going to tell you.

In the past I did look at pornography. I had avoided it for quite some time because of the strong pull it has. Most men are addicted to it before they even view it. Watching sexual interactions triggers something in most men. If you have ever seen it and have enjoyed it for just one second, you are guilty. I am aware of the danger of pop-up messages on the Internet. They can lead someone to images they had no intentions of seeing. What you do at that point determines your true character. By continuing on, a person commits visual adultery. *Matthew 5:28-29 NKJV: "I say to you that whoever looks at a woman to lust for her has already committed adultery with her in his heart. If your right eye causes you to sin, pluck it out and cast it from you, for it is more profitable that one of your members perish, than for your whole body to be cast into hell."* I failed the character test. You can justify your actions all you want, but Jesus makes it pretty clear: *"Stop!"*

Those images of the pole dancers coalesced in my mind. The delicate balance of the teeter-totter hovering in the neutral position was about to be slammed down by fleshly desire. Once the Internet became an instant access port, pornography use skyrocketed. Something that was kept behind closed doors now was mainstream. A couple clicks of the keys and right in front of my eyes was any kind of sexual act I wanted to view.

I told my wife that I was struggling with sexual temptation, but our current communication level was not conducive to any assistance in this area. Thinking about this transgression is heartbreaking. The images that I had put out of my mind were resurfacing. Just the act of talking about them shuffles them up the memory stack. This area has caused so many people to stumble. Hopefully my vulnerability will help others resist this treacherous downhill slope. The merry-go-round once initiated continues on a redundant exercise of self-gratification. In your mind, you can make all kinds of justifications. That is because you know it is wrong and you should not be partaking in it.

After each round of gratification, guilt instantly sets in. Then the images you already consumed begin to stimulate you once again. Eventually, that leads to visually consuming more images. Another round of self-gratification and the merry-go-round continues, all the while accumulating more trash in your mind that you have to deal with. You are a *fool* if you think this does not have a considerable cost. This endless merry-go-round behavior continued for several days. I pleaded with God to help me overcome it. Finally, through God's Word and my watching some Godly men on YouTube, the beast was caged up once again.

I discovered a new wrinkle that the Internet offers for the propagation of prostitution. When I would be viewing porn on my computer, pop-ups of solicitation would appear. Not only that, the pop-ups would state the distance that they were from me. While I was looking at these images, the pop-up would say, "Hi, my name is Juicy. I am 25, and these are my body measurements. I want to..." Then it would say 2.4 miles away. This just shows you how are far our society has descended into the pit. By the grace of God, I never clicked on one of those or pursued them in the physical realm. The reason I say this is I am sure I thought about it, especially with the accelerated rate of decay in my relationship with my wife.

During this time, battles were raging in my mind. Many nights, I would walk by the ocean in the pitch dark. Images would dart in and out of my mind. Demonic darkness would descend upon me like sheets of rain. Mixed in with that were pinpricks of brilliant light. Each was trying to extinguish the other. I would beg God to help me. My personal life was falling apart. The situation I was putting my wife through was unbearable for her, consequently she could not contain her emotions. The flood of tears that she shed swept up my daughter. The once-solid relationship was damaged and taking on water quickly. Finally, it had gotten to a point where both my wife and daughter chose not to communicate with me.

I shoulder a major part of the responsibility, because there were many things that I did wrong. Instead of assuring my wife that everything was fine, I adopted the opposite approach. The mental toughness that I exhibited throughout the years was displayed through dominance, not in a loving, kind way that would have helped resolve the issues. The realization that God was behind these questions became an intense area of focus. The personal revelations that I discovered from individuals were profound. I will highlight a few of their responses to give you a sense of what I am talking about.

By far the most frequent answer to the question "What was the worst thing that has ever happened to you?" was the Pulse nightclub massacre. I would have been surprised if it had been anything other than that. The most unexpected answer to this question came from a man named John. He had been in a train accident that killed his entire family. Not only that, everyone else on the train was killed. John was the only survivor. Thankfully, his grandparents adopted him. That was the answer he gave to the question "What was the best thing that happened to you?" His situation resulted in significant psychological challenges. He told me that he had needed years of counseling.

My listening to these heartfelt stories was the way that God started to pry open my understanding. I began to realize that any prejudice I held toward the LGBTQ group or any other was not based in God's love. Christians have become quite versed in condemning while continuing in the sin of gluttony or something else. Of course, if they would read the Scriptures, they would know that we are not to judge those outside of the church, but those in the church. *1 Corinthians 5:12-13 NKJV: "For what have I to do judging those also who are outside? Do you not judge those who are inside? But those who are outside God judges. Therefore put away from yourselves that evil person."* How dare we sit by some of the worst sinners every week in church and never hold them accountable. We may easily turn our glare of indignation on those not in the church.

When we choose not to demonstrate love, we have already failed. This was one of Jesus's greatest commands. That does not mean that I can compromise any part of what the Bible says about sin. The choices that we make when we violate Scripture are sinful. You might not like it, because heck, there are some things you have a hard time with. Eventually, you realize that God knows a whole a lot more than you do. I still had not surrendered enough of myself to come to that conclusion. My next training ground was in a soup kitchen.

After going through the necessary screening process, I became a volunteer at the kitchen. The program was centered on homeless people, and it offered a variety of services. The first opportunity I had to interact was on a Saturday morning. There was a coat, hat and glove distribution event. I was in charge of the line of people who came to receive the clothing, helping control the flow. This gave me some time to interact with many of the recipients. When I got a signal from the people manning the tables, I would send another half-dozen of the recipients to them. While we were waiting for the event to start, there were probably fifty people in line.

All of a sudden, I heard two loudmouth women approaching with a pair of pit bulls. Everyone in the line cringed at their arrival. They were like scared antelope that had just sensed a couple of approaching lioness. The women were roaring curse words and condemnation at most everyone. Normally, I would have jumped into my suit of flesh and started my own barrage of return fire. These were large gals, so my response would have been, "You couple of fat b******, go on and shut your mouths." I am not offering this as a consolation prize to myself, but normally I would always stand up for someone who was being bullied, except when I was the instigator. Sadly, I have to admit, with my family I usually was the instigator. Today was different, and God had another plan.

The first thought that entered my mind was, "They have been terribly hurt." The younger of the two women was the launchpad for most of the verbal assaults. "Who was this thinking this thought?" I wondered. The response was so foreign to me. I would never let anybody slide with that kind of behavior, except myself. No matter how hard I tried to be upset with this situation, empathy, I guess, won the wrestling match. A few days later it would become crystal clear why I had responded that way.

Another situation I encountered that day was of a different nature. A group of volunteers had organized this event, possibly from a local church or outreach organization. I watched them arrive in three or four separate vehicles. The majority of the volunteers looked like they were high school age. Since I was the official line captain, I was eager for the event to start. Watching everyone chitchat and get their hot chocolate and take selfies until nearly twenty minutes after the starting time agitated me. When the event finally got underway, my irritation continued.

Many of the volunteers were taking selfies and pictures of the homeless people. I was sure those photos would find their way to the volunteers' favorite social media platform and become humble boasts. Why did this bother me so much? I continued to deliberate until God prompted me with this: "If you did not like what you saw here, go look in the mirror at what that guy has done."

"Yes, God, you are right," I thought. Countless times I used situations to draw attention to myself. Even if it was not deserved but could have put me in a good light, I would take it. More times than not, when we find an irritating characteristic in someone, it is because we share that trait and do not want to admit it.

The following Monday, I was assigned to the outdoor patio area at the soup kitchen. Several benches lined the perimeter and others were positioned down through the center. Roughly forty people could sit there. The patio connected to the soup kitchen and was a congregating place throughout the day. The first day I was there, I wore the appropriate identification badge. People reacted to the badge the way they do to the bright colored stripes of a poisonous frog: It repelled them. The second day, I slipped the badge into my pocket as soon as I walked outside onto the patio. Also, the night before, I picked up some scruffier cloths to blend in better. Most of the people did not remember me from the day before.

Within the first half-hour, people were asking me if I was homeless. Being a thousand miles away from home, I was able to say, "At the moment, yes." I learned quickly that the customary way of starting a conversation did not suit this situation. Standing next to someone and not saying anything for five minutes or so was more or less the introduction. After that, some sort of conversation could begin. I ended up asking twelve homeless people the four questions. Many of them had descended into the clutches of addiction. Some went through horrific experiences in which they had no control.

One of the women told me how she was brutally raped at thirteen years old. She had to have reconstructive surgery. Other situations in her life also caused her great suffering. She was a drug addict and warned anyone who was considering trying drugs not to do it. A gentleman who I interviewed had been an assistant chaplain. He also had owned a construction company and had a wife and family. His addiction cost him everything. I could tell he was bitter and remorseful. He was mad at himself for his inability to escape. Seeing the hopelessness in his eyes was troubling. The battle inside him had raged on for so long that I believed he was waving the white flag. He knew if he focused on Jesus, he could be set free.

On the third day, I spoke with the young lady who had been so venomous toward others. This was the one I had empathy for. Based on her behavior, I never would have felt that way before. She arrived at the patio the same she had the previous Saturday: like a roaring lioness stalking her prey. Most of the benches were full when she arrived, yet she just kicked people off where she thought she should sit. She was with the same woman who accompanied her the other day. Turns out they were mother and daughter. When they nestled into their seats, a twenty-foot radius cleared around them. No one wanted to be within striking distance. I watched and listened for several minutes.

I slowly approached and sat next to the boisterous one. She gave me a sneer of disgust, as if I were violating her space. I waited patiently for a few minutes then placed my hand on her shoulder. Her head spun in my direction, like she was a honey badger whose attention was caught by a delectable meal. Her eyes contacted mine, and I was not sure if I was going to lose some of my fingers. I quickly said, "I would like to ask you some questions, and I bet you would have some great answers." Her lips came unfurled, and her teeth retreated.

Her name was Sasha. The four questions revealed much. When asked, "What advice would you give about life?" she said, "Get along with others and work." She had no success in either of these areas. The best thing in her life was having her baby girl. Now came the real eye-opener. The reason God had me respond to her initial introduction was about to be revealed. The worst thing that happened to her was that she was raped at five years old. Her mother, sitting nearby, confirmed this. Not only that, she caught her boyfriend sodomizing her dog. I could hardly believe what I was hearing. When I asked her the final question, "How can humanity love one another better?" she said, "You have to love yourself first." Eventually I interviewed hundreds of people. She was the only one who answered the fourth question that way.

Listening to her, I could barely keep my composure. I rarely cried and was always a tough guy. A tear trickled down my cheek, and I wondered what got in my eye to cause that. The reality was that something was getting into my heart. I had to remove myself from the situation, because I thought the tears would come like April showers. Over in the corner, I gathered my composure and continued to watch Sasha. She stopped talking and was no longer making rude and obscene comments to anyone. For nearly an hour she did not speak. Finally, I went up to her and said, "It is not your fault. God loves you." She had tears in her eyes. Probably for the first time, her defenses were down, and maybe just a drop of love got in.

I now knew something definitely was going on inside me. My awareness of others outside of my little selfish world was expanding. While my relationship with family back home was crumbling, in the outside world, it was blossoming. After the experience at the soup kitchen, I felt certain God had inspired this journey and these questions. The pride and ego had not been shaken loose enough just yet. The string of stupidity continued. My resistance to reconciliation with my wife was growing stronger. I could not imagine her responding poorly to the magnificent way that God was using me. How great it was that I would drive all the way to Florida to help bring understanding to these people. *Proverbs 25:14 NKJV: "Whoever falsely boasts of giving is like clouds and wind without rain."* That is more like it—I was still just a bag of wind.

Pride is like the bully who wants to take cuts in the line, muscling its way to the top of any opportunity it gets. Only when we are aware of our true position with God can we kick it out of line. The thing is, it always tries to muscle its way back in. My encounter with Sasha revealed God's plan to put out the consuming fire of pride in me. The lone tear that ran down my cheek cracked open my broken soul. What had been held back by pride and self-righteousness was now beginning to flow. The simple tears became God's weapon of choice. He used them to usher in a cascading effect on my being. Finally, there was a sun, beaming hope that change could occur. Thank you, Jesus, for your persistence.

CHAPTER 14

———

THE EMERGING PROCESS OF LEARNING ABOUT OTHER people's lives was the pivotal point. A simple investment of five to twenty minutes per person paid huge dividends. I interviewed nearly one hundred people and quickly was able to discern much more than what the questions revealed. There were many ways that I screwed it up though. Since Jesus is the best representative of love that humanity has ever been exposed to, He should have been the focal point. In my great wisdom, I tried to keep Jesus out of it. I would even make specific statements indicating I was promoting love and acceptance. The funny thing is that God would put a Christian in my life almost daily to remind me of the true nature of my mission.

I was not smart enough to heed God's counsel. He would blatantly put someone in my path with the right answers. Mike was in the vacation village, and he was my thirty-ninth interview. These were Mike's answers to my questions: 1) What advice would you give about how to live life? "Live with the fruit of the spirit." 2) What was the best thing that ever happened to you? "Obtaining salvation through Jesus Christ." 3) What was the worst thing that ever happened to you? "Losing loved ones." 4) How can humanity love one another better? "We must master forgiveness and compassion." Apparently, during this conversation, my listening skills were not engaged, and because of this I continued to suffer the detriments of my ignorance.

After the 2016 presidential election, lots of division and strife were brewing in our country, so I reasoned that I had this wonderful solution. My pride was not going to give up easily. The gift of the three extra questions and the order in which they were asked came from God. My pride plagiarized from the rightful owner, God, and I instead took credit. *Proverbs 12:22 NKJV: "Lying lips are an abomination to the Lord, those who deal truthfully are his delight."* I will reveal how that happened, but before I do, I want to share a couple more of the encounters I had. The more interviews I did, the more predictable were the answers. I learned how to be a good listener when I wanted to, and I fine-tuned my awareness of subtle body language cues.

I interviewed a couple, presumably husband and wife, and their two sons. The boys were probably between five and ten years old; the mom and dad were somewhere around thirty. We spoke at a yacht club's restaurant. Due to the content of their answers, I will just refer to them as interview number thirty-five. There was tension at the table the moment I sat down. They were getting ready to order their meal. I insisted that I could leave and that they did not have to do the interview. With a snarl and an arched eyebrow, the wife said, "No, that is fine. We will just do it." I asked the first question, "What advice would you give about how to live life?" She looked at her husband with a piercing glare.

Had she been Superman, she would have burned holes right through him.

Glancing at her two sons and tipping her head as to include herself, she said, "Do not take things for granted and enjoy what you have." The grimace that she fired at her husband said, "Why did you cheat on us, you piece of s***?" Do you think I am jumping to conclusions too quickly? Hold on.

Next question: "What was the best thing that ever happened to you?" She stared down at the table with a blank look. Her inability to answer that question spoke volumes. After a bit of uncomfortable time for everyone, she looked at her husband and said, "Maybe you should answer that one." She said it very sarcastically.

Her mind was completely occupied with the treacherous act. She was the only person who didn't answer that question. I was surprised she did not at least say, "Having my two sons." The clouds of despair that she was in did not allow her to see beyond the darkness.

When I asked, "What was the worst thing that ever happened to you?" while flashing a concerned look toward one of her sons, she answered, "Having a child misdiagnosed in the hospital."

I asked the fourth question, "How can humanity love one another better?" She looked me straight in the eye and said, "Be kind to strangers, and take one day at a time." This was an obvious reference to the struggle she had each day trying to overcome the circumstances. The unforgiveness was eating her up. God was giving me a glimpse of what the Holy Spirit's discernment looked like. There was just one huge obstacle: me.

I was able to interview policemen, EMTs, firefighters, people who were very poor and homeless, and people who were very rich. God had specifically guided me to the Pulse nightclub because I was deficient in the measure of love I demonstrated toward the LGBT crowd. Now there was another group I showed deficiency of love toward who God wanted me to visit. I contacted a local Muslim Iman and told him about my research. I asked if I could come to the mosque and interview some people. As God would have it, an event was planned and would take place in three days. I ended up interviewing twenty-two Muslims. God did not put me in this situation to challenge their faith. He put me there to demonstrate love and compassion.

One thing that surprised me was how many answered that the best thing that happened to them was being born Muslim. Far fewer of the Christians I interviewed pointed to Jesus Christ, and more pointed to the things of the world. I think that is pretty telling of the strength of our Christian faith in this country. I want you to be honest with yourself for a second, because your eternal destination hinges on it. If I ask you this question, *"What is the best thing that ever happened to you?" pause a few moments until you formulate an answer.* If you call yourself a Christian and your first response is not "Following Jesus Christ as my Lord and Savior," then I am highly skeptical about your eternal destination.

You could make all the excuses you want, and none would surprise me, because I have used them all. Jesus makes it very clear: If He is not number one in your life, then most likely you fall into this category. *Matthew 7:21-23 NKJV: "Not everyone who says to me, Lord, Lord, shall enter the king-*

dom of heaven, but he who does the will of my father in heaven. Many will say to me in that day, Lord, Lord, have we not prophesied in your name, cast out demons in your name, and done many wonders in your name? And then I will declare to them, I never knew you, depart from me, you who practice lawlessness." I do not care how many preachers have told you something different from this; Jesus tells it like it is.

There was a Muslim woman, interview number sixty-one, who gave a unique answer to question number four, "What can humanity due to love one another better?" She said, "Get close to your enemy, walk in their shoes, then maybe they will not be your enemy anymore." That reminds me of something Jesus said. *Luke 6:27-28 NKJV: "But I say to you who hear, love your enemies, do good to those who hate you, bless those who curse you, and pray for those who spitefully use you."* How many Christians would have answered this question the way this Muslim did? Many of the Muslim responses reflected kindness and consideration. Just to be clear, my faith in Jesus Christ has not budged one bit. Were the Muslims' responses sincere and heartfelt? Only God knows.

One of the people I interviewed, Faizan, watched his uncle get blown to bits in front of his eyes by a bomb blast in Iran. He was only a teenager. That is a horrible memory to have to live with for the rest of your life. There were many stories of people treating these Muslims in a hateful way. I do not care what justification you think you have. The moment we operate outside of love, we are being disobedient to Jesus. I am not getting argumentative here, just presenting the clear facts as they are found in the Bible.

Here are the responses from two Muslim boys. One was

seven years old; the other was nine: "What advice would you give about how to live life?" The seven-year-old reasoned "Save your stuff for when you need it," and nine-year-old stated, "Get a job and get money."

"What is the best thing that ever happened to you?" The younger one said, "Going to a party," and the older recalled his trip to Disney World in Orlando.

"What was the worst thing that ever happened to you?" The seven-year-old was sad when he could not go outside to play, and the nine-year-old was distraught when his lava lamp fell off the dresser and broke.

"How can people love each other better?" The younger boy said, "To be nice," and the other boy said, "Not to be mean." I dare to say that these are answers that most American children would give. It is time for us to agree on our similarities and treat each other with respect. Only out of our love for one another will non-believers take a serious look at our faith in Jesus. Why in the world would they want to be part of a hateful, judgmental and self-righteous group? We need to do a much better job representing what Jesus modeled.

Many of the comments have become clear to me only because the Holy Spirit has revealed the true nature of who I was. Now it is time for me to reveal some of the facts about how badly I handled the situation with my wife. God was giving me a crash course in empathy and compassion acquisition. Somewhere around the one hundredth interview, I had the sense of God whispering in my mind. I had just completed a heart-wrenching interview, and part of that person's feelings had become my feelings. It reminded me of one of the books I wrote. The awareness floated gently into my soul. The imprint I had from God was, "The love you are feeling is the love I have for everyone."

God planted that thought deep in my mind, and it took root. Wherever I went, I looked at people differently. Their outward appearance diminished in importance. I realized I was seeing spiritual beings. Part of me was being stirred, and something was awakening that had never surfaced before. The other part of me was being cynical, malicious and destructive. My relationship with my wife was not improving. In fact, it continued to deteriorate. Before I made the journey home, my pride had seized the opportunity to put the spotlight on myself in an unorthodox way.

Phase one of the plan was probably inspired by God. Gaining more compassion for the less fortunate was the intended outcome. When I went to a Goodwill store to buy some old clothes and a gray wig, I had an interesting encounter with a woman as I was exiting the store. Was it an angel? You decide. The first thing she said to me was, "You are supposed to go home and be with your wife."

This took me by surprise, so I asked her, "Do you know why I am here?"

She responded, "Why yes, I do. You are here to talk to people."

"What people?" I questioned.

"All kinds," she replied, waving her arm in front of her. Then she reaffirmed, "It is time for you to go home."

Needless to say, I was shocked by the exchange.

I had not eaten or shaved for seventeen days. Taking on the appearance of a homeless man was pretty easy. I used suntan oil and a chocolate bar to make my skin look dirty and my hair greasy. The scientific experiment, as I labeled it, was to see just how invisible I would become to the public. There was one significant twist. I made a sign that read, "Free money; help yourself," and then filled a vegetable colander with a few hundred dollars and went to a vacation area where many wealthy people were walking around.

Most of the people were downright rude to me. No matter how many times I said, "Read the sign" and pointed to the money, it did not register in their minds. They were brainwashed to such an extent that they could not even read a couple of words. People would say, "I do not have any money." I would say, "I do not want any money." Then I would say, "Read the sign." They would get mad, turn their pockets inside out, and say, "I told you I do not have any money." What a bunch of liars.

This was a very wealthy community. This experience made me take a hard look at myself. These people who were so inconsiderate and unkind were really reflections of the way I had acted many times. The tactic that I would use most often was just to ignore people. Jesus gives us a pretty stern warning concerning this. *Matthew 25:45-46 NKJV: "Then he will answer them, saying, assuredly, I say to you, inasmuch as you did not do it to one of the least of these, you did not do it to me. And these will go away into everlasting punishment, but the righteous into eternal life."*

Most of the people who I encountered probably treated their dogs better than they treated me. When I pulled the wig up and told them I was doing a scientific experiment, they scurried off in a huff.

God had concluded phase one of Empathy and Compassion 101, but I decided to continue on to phase whatever by promoting myself and drawing attention to my efforts. I contacted a TV station. Pretty stupid, I know. God probably shook his head and thought, "You have got to be kidding me!" Except that He knew it was going to happen. I did the TV interview with my wig and homeless attire, but I did not give my name. I kinda, sorta tried to be anonymous, but not really. When I mentioned to my wife and daughter what I did, they identified it right away. Why did I pollute something that could have had significant impact?

After I had forced the spotlight on myself once again, I felt it was time to return home. My wife and I now had a go-between, because our communication had deteriorated to such a point. My son had become chief counselor for both of us—not a position parents should ever put their children in. There was a bright spot in my home situation. My daughter had been the unwilling recipient of much negativity. Particularly, my weeping wife pegged me as guilty without a trial. She was mostly right. If I view myself as the spiritual leader and head of the household, I had failed miserably. My daughter could not understand how people could talk to me so openly, how they could share deep, dark secrets with a total stranger.

I asked her if she would give me a couple hours of her time. I returned home and picked her up and went to a local mall. We were going to ask the questions to random individuals so that she could experience it herself. She was shocked when she learned from the first person we asked, a twenty-four-year-old man, that he had a genetic heart defect and would need a transplant within the next twelve months.

The young man who was with him, an eighteen-year-older, had attempted suicide the year before. We talked to a young woman who had just found out her father was going to prison for four years. Several others held back tears as they answered our questions. Probably for the first time in her life, my daughter saw me cry, as I was overcome with emotion while speaking with these total strangers. Imagine that.

This was on December 24. When we left the mall and returned to our vehicle, my daughter looked at me with tears running down her cheeks and said, "I get it. I had no idea." These stories were hard to hear, but I was thankful that she and I were together to hear them. During our thirty-five-minute drive home we soberly reflected on what had happened. A few minutes before arriving home, we got into a disagreement. I had plans to stay at the house, though I had been gone for three weeks. But this argument hardened my heart, and I dropped my daughter off and sped away.

I was heartbroken and cried nearly the entire way to the hotel. How could she turn on me after what we had experienced together? At least that was the lie I was telling myself. Really, it had been a lifetime of my not doing a good job as a father or spiritual leader. I spent Christmas Eve at a hotel with a few strangers. My strong will, pride and arrogance were not willing to surrender yet. My son called me and could not believe I was staying at a hotel, thirty miles from my home. He said, "Dad, I will meet you at the house tomorrow morning so that we can all talk." How much of it was my stubbornness? How much of it was Satan trying to derail God's plan to awaken me? I cried out to God. I felt like I could not take the unsettled life much more. I had gone nearly three weeks without food, and I was desperately struggling to find answers.

My mind was a battleground throughout the night. Demonic forces were swimming in and out of my consciousness. I could see dark shadows twisting and turning, rolling around in my mind. Flashes of brilliant light would intercede. They were acting as beacons of hope and defenders of my mind. By the time I woke up in the morning, I had a sense of clarity. Everything seemed clear, and the mission instructions had been handed down. Marching orders had been given. Now it was up to me to take full responsibility for all the discord that I had sowed with my wife.

God told me, "You are a grown man. You do not need your son to be your counselor. Go home and tell your wife and daughter you are sorry. Take 100 percent responsibility for what happened. Be loving, kind and gentle. You will be going on part two of your journey. In six days, you will be leaving for another three weeks. Now it is up to you."

With that thought pasted in my mind, I packed everything up and left the hotel. I was not sure how it was going to go when I got home. Tears ran down my cheeks, blurring my vision as I drove. Fortunately, it was Christmas morning, so there was very little traffic on the road.

I knew that something was changing drastically inside me. Every time I viewed other humans, I felt different about them. They became much more valuable to me, but in the sense of what they could do for me or how I can benefit from them. It was more in the sense of how valuable their lives were. Somehow, my view of humanity had been enhanced substantially.

CHAPTER 15

———

I ARRIVED AT MY HOUSE MID-MORNING ON CHRIST-
mas day. The only way to stop the downward spiral of my
relationship with my wife was to take complete responsibility
for everything that happened. The awareness of the Holy
Spirit had become more prevalent in my life. Following the
Spirit's direction would lead to a better path. My daughter,
my wife and I sat down for a meal together for the first time
in over three weeks. I confessed many of my wrong actions.
No longer was I bound and determined to lay some of the
blame on my wife, at least not at this time.

Thankfully, the presence of the Holy Spirit was with me.
This prevented me from being a right fighter and pointing
out someone else's flaws, whether it was deserved or not.
Usually, that is just a tactic to shift responsibility to someone
else. I was well versed in that sly attack and used it several
times against my wife.

It felt good to be back home, and I was ready to release
the roller coaster of emotions. Not long after I got home, my
thoughts started to take on a more selfish nature. I was
completely sincere with the things that I had shared with
my family. Seeing my wife again aroused thoughts of inti-

macy. But I had hurt her with the things I had said, and that was a significant roadblock.

Some of my words and actions had a selfish slant to them. I knew full well that I would be leaving in a few days, and I wanted to have as much sex in that short time as I could. I had alluded to the fact that I had viewed pornography while I was gone. I did not go into much detail and certainly was not at the point of admitting that it was as bad as committing adultery. The affections that I demonstrated toward my wife were mostly sincere, however, I knew in my heart that personal conquest was at least some of my motive. An element of manipulation advanced my desires by a few days.

When God shows us who we really are, it can be painful to realize the depth of our selfishness. At the time, I would have described my actions as those of a loving husband trying to romance his wife, but the Holy Spirit will not let me off the hook without divulging the entire truth. Something else happened while I was away. Satan is constantly looking for weaknesses in our defenses or entry points to get us off track. The time I was giving into the desires of the flesh and watching pornography, I also was disobedient in another area. God had made it clear to me that my name was not to appear on the books. But somehow, during this period, I allowed my name to appear on the cover of one of the books.

I was working with an assistant on the final cover. In big bold letters on the bottom was my name. Whether I would admit it, pride welled up inside of me. I sent a copy of the artwork to my son and asked his opinion. Thank God for his boldness. He immediately cautioned, "What is up with your name on the book? I thought you said God wanted you to be invisible?"

Of course, he was right, and I admitted that I should not have allowed that to happen. My sinful behavior weakened my resolve. The enemy was not finished with this situation just yet.

After talking to my son, I prayed about what I should do. I knew that my name was not to be on the books, so I believed that God had inspired me to use a different approach. The idea seemed to make perfect sense to me: Add a T to your name. Strategically placed, it changed the pronunciation. I reasoned that God had to be the one who inspired me to do so. The T represented the cross, and by adding it I was putting Christ first. Sounds pretty good, right? On top of that, the placement of the letter even made the name sound humble. I was sure I had it all figured out and was crediting God for the marvelous insight. *1 Timothy 4:1-2 NKJV: "Now the Spirit expressly says in later times some will depart from the faith, giving heed to deceiving spirits and doctrines of demons, speaking lies in hypocrisy, having their own conscience seared with a hot iron."*

The first time I saw the new name sprawled across the bottom of the cover, I realized I had been deceived. All of the seemingly positive spiritual reasons I was telling myself were lies. God had made it clear that my name was not to be on the book. Adding a T made no difference. I felt foolish seeing the new name in print. I immediately repented and realized I had been duped by the devil. He will sprinkle as much truth as necessary to convince us that a lie is truth. I felt confident that God was allowing me to hide my name in plain sight. When I finally realized the reality of the situation, it was embarrassing to think how much pride was still roaming the hallways of my mind.

In preparation for phase two of my trip, my pride would sneak in an attack. The beast would take large bites out of what God was intending to do and use it to fill its own stomach of ego. The time was suitable for version 2.0 of my empathy and compassion training to start. I was about to embark on another three-week journey. The nation had just gone through one of the most hate-filled election cycles ever. There seemed to be a never-ending news cycle of negative stories and comments. Since "I" had discovered this great disarming mechanism disguised as four questions, I could probably save the country.

God had intended 2.0 as a reinforcing tool to solidify my empathy and compassion for others. I specifically felt as though I was to visit several college campuses. Gaining a perspective on a certain demographic could prove to be valuable. I had noticed in my previous interviews that younger people tended to give more consistent responses, particularly to the fourth question, "How can humanity love one another better?" Before we roll out on this journey, I will explain how my ego hijacked certain aspects of the mission.

I had this grandiose idea that I could somehow get Barack Obama, Donald Trump and Bill Clinton to give their responses to the questions. If they all agreed, it could serve as a healing catalyst for our country. The unique thing about these questions is that the answers reveal so many similarities between humans. Maybe if people recognized their similarities, cooperation could be more attainable. I will never know how close I came to being shot, but certainly my actions got me into some precarious situations.

Phase one of my journey ended on Christmas day. Phase two started on New Year's Eve, with my first stop being the University of Michigan campus. After that stop, I decided to hit as many college campuses as I could on my way to New York.

I interviewed thirteen people at U of M. The similarities between answers to question four convinced me to investigate further. During the journey I stopped at four more college campuses: Ohio State, Pittsburgh, Penn State and Harvard. The majority of the answers to question four, "How can humanity love one another better?" were "compassion, listening, be more forgiving, be honest," and other variations on that theme. The good news was that most of the answers focused on empathy and compassion. The bad news was that on every campus I visited, people were immersed in their phones and other handheld devices, paying little attention to the outside world.

I am not sure how someone is going to radically change the world when they are relying on a phone to interact with others. I have some thoughts on the disintegrating nature of our social fabric. Actions that we initiated in this generation will have profound ramifications, and they are already being felt.

Daily, God would put a Christian influencer in my path. I was still denying Jesus by not acknowledging that my mission was about loving one another. In retrospect, that is exactly what Jesus was all about. It seems silly now. Even a grade schooler could have made that connection. *Matthew*

7:12 NKJV: "Therefore, whatever you want men to do to you, do also to them, for this is the law and the prophets."

Jackson, from Ohio State, gave it to me pretty straight. 1) Living life: "Living with the vision to meet other people's needs before myself." 2) Best thing: "Being saved by Jesus Christ." 3) Worst thing: "Nothing, I have lived a blessed life." 4) Loving humanity: "Radically loving God first."

Consistently, God would put people in front of me to clearly speak the truth. I had not relinquished full control yet, so I was recording information, but only on occasion would it sink in. Compiling a book about the various responses to the questions would be easy. I literally did hundreds of interviews. The outlier answers are most interesting.

The final college campus I visited was Harvard. An experience that took place there is hard to talk about. The many despicable actions that I have already revealed probably have prepared you to hear about it. I am not proud of any of these horrifying behaviors that I have demonstrated. The fact of the matter is, they reveal my sinful and fallen nature. The Holy Spirit is now in charge of my life. Full surrender means full obedience. I tussled with God a bit over the importance of such an admission. He won.

On this journey, the relationship with my wife became exponentially better. Realizing how much of a loser it made me feel to watch the sexual acts of others, I vowed with the help of God not to do it again. That sounds far creepier than watching pornography, but let us just be honest and state it as it is. There are far more graphic ways of describing these readily available videos to pollute the mind. The really sad thing is that we justify it, and I am including myself in that category. I am a fool, and so are you if you think any of those justifications work with God. The only time looking at such images is acceptable is when they are of your spouse. The moment any other images are introduced for sexual gratification, you have crossed the line. That is why it is so important not to have any sexual images stored in your mind, unless they are of your spouse.

Warning: mature content! I woke up in the hotel room with an erection that would not go away, so I indulged myself, using images from the pornography I had viewed as stimulation. In essence, I reached a climax thinking about other women. *1 Peter 2:11 NKJV: "Beloved, I beg you a sojourners and pilgrims, abstain from fleshly lust which war against the soul."* According to Jesus, I had committed adultery for lusting after another woman. All of you Christian men who think this is okay, *you are in big trouble, and God knows you by name.*

This may seem like a foolish thing to draw attention to, but God does not think so. He made sure that this memory would not escape me.

Later that day, while I was walking around Harvard Square, I was surprised by the number of homeless people in the area. I walked into a large building that had several small food cafés. In the central hub was a collection of tables and chairs for people to sit and eat the food they purchased. Along one edge was a section of high-top tables with barstools. Only one person sat in this section, and he appeared to be homeless. He was very scruffy looking and had a large bag of gummy worms. He had his back to me, and I stopped several feet away, because it seemed like he was talking to someone. He wasn't saying anything coherent, just garbled words. When I approached his table, he had a handful of gummy worms in his hand. He dropped them and stared right at me. I will never forget what he said.

Warning: mature content! After he looked me over from top to bottom, he said this: "Look at you, jacking off all over yourself. You are quite an example."

He then went back to speaking gibberish. I became invisible to him. I stood there, shocked at what had just happened and what he said. Finally, I walked outside the building, but then turned around and walked right back in. I was gone for only seconds. I sensed that I had just encountered an angel, or a demon. I wasn't sure which. I could not find Mr. Gummy Worms anywhere. There were only two exits from the building. Quickly, I moved from one to the other and even walked around the block. He had disappeared. I feel sorry and embarrassed to admit such things, but I could not get away from the fact that I was supposed to tell about this incident.

The big three who I had identified to ask the questions were now in my sights. I traveled to Chappaqua, New York, where the Clintons lived. Within twenty-four hours, I had located the Secret Service house and the Clintons' residence. The Secret Service house had easily visible cameras positioned in many locations. I believe there were seven black Chevy Suburbans with tinted windows and government plates. They all had little satellite antennas on the top of them. I sat in the adjacent parking lot. I am sure they were monitoring my activities, because I sat there for nearly half an hour.

Many times in my life, my boldness has outweighed my wisdom. Finally, I got out of the vehicle and walked right up to the house and knocked on the door. To my surprise, somebody answered it. The gentleman was courteous and actually listened to what I had to say. I tried to hand him a sheet of paper with the questions and contact information. He politely said that he could not take it and dismissed himself from our conversation. A few hours later, I located the Clintons' residence. Again, I did a similar stupid move by approaching their house. I did not get far before I was confronted by a Secret Service agent. Most likely, he had already been alerted about some crazy guy and his sheet of paper.

The reason that I am telling you about these situations is so that you realize how lofty my thoughts of myself were and what I thought I could achieve under my own power. This was only two months after a very contentious election.

After I left Chappaqua, I went to New York City. I stayed eight days and went to Trump Tower three times. I was surprised that I could even get in the building. Several times, I spoke with Secret Service agents. The security there was considerable. Media members were positioned outside the elevators at all times. Everyone was hoping to get a glimpse of Trump or some other recognizable figure. I asked one of the Secret Service agents what would happen if I stood in front of the elevators and addressed the media.

He strongly advised against it. I explained to him about the importance of restoring some sort of unity in our country. "We owe it to our children," I reasoned. For a moment, something sank into his tough exterior. Then I walked away.

About twenty minutes later, I did exactly what I asked about doing. Amazingly, though I was quickly flanked by Secret Service agents, I allowed to talk for a few minutes. My heart was sincere about trying to do something right, but my arrogance far outweighed any authority I had in the situation. I was as interested in drawing attention to myself as I was in drawing attention to the intense unrest in the country. I do want to mention one thing about some college students from England who I interviewed.

Many of the students I interviewed in the college towns had self-centered answers to question one, "What advice would you give about how to live life?" They included "Do whatever you want," "Live life to the fullest," "Take risks, because you only live once," and so forth. The question prompted similar responses from the students from England, but with one significant difference. Nearly half of the students added this to their initial thoughts: "as long as it does not cause harm to anyone else." Only the students from England added that sentiment to their answers. Just a point to ponder, and probably one that deserves more investigation.

After my impromptu press conference at Trump Tower, I headed to Washington, D.C., for the inauguration. I had sent a request to the White House concerning the questions. I received a response, probably the same one sent to thousands of other people. I continued my same bold behavior, going places I should not and relying on my own abilities to achieve spectacular things (*not*). I basically spent three weeks so God could show me how ridiculous my adventures were at times. Some were still part of His plan for me to better understand empathy and compassion.

Many protests were taking place in Washington, D.C., and I got to interact with people on both sides. I was also there for Martin Luther King Day and marched in the front row of a demonstration the entire distance. A black woman, Kayla, came up to me and gave me a hug. She said, "I can see it in you that Jesus has got you on a mission."

The love I felt from the people at the event was spectacular. Tears flowed down my cheeks on several occasions. They made me feel like part of their family. Maybe that was why I felt prompted to attend a black church a few months later. Even this experience can now be placed in its rightful position for what God was trying to teach me. God placed several other people on my path. Kayla told me not to deny Jesus. At the time, I was not fully aware of how much I was doing that. Until we are completely surrendered to His Lordship, some part of our life is still denying him.

Take an honest look at yourself today. Do not be a stubborn bonehead and waste many years like I have. Surrender completely to Jesus, and He will help you remove the things that are detrimental. Do not be resistant, because it is not worth it. *John 15: 1–7 NKJV: "I am the true vine, and my father is the vine dresser. Every branch in me that does not bear fruit he takes away, and every branch that bears fruit he prunes, that it may bear more fruit. You are already clean because of the word which I have spoken to you abide in me, and I in you. As the branch cannot bear fruit of itself, unless it abides in the vine, neither can you, unless you abide in me. I am the vine, you are the branches. He who abides in me, and I in him, bears much fruit, for without me you can do nothing. If anyone does not abide in me, he is cast out as a branch and is withered, and they gather them and throw them into the fire, and they are burned. If you abide in me, and my words abide in you, you will ask what you desire, and it shall be done for you."*

On my drive back home, I had much to ponder. I was coming to the realization that God must have a better plan than I do. The culmination of countless unfulfilled pride quests had begun a domino effect inside me. God was about to do some major pruning. Nearly my entire branch was infested with pride. One major ingredient was lacking within me. God had to buckle down pretty hard on me to get me to understand. Because of my stubborn nature and self-righteous behavior, the discipline was completely necessary. I was about to learn what the fear of God meant in a huge way.

CHAPTER 16

―――――

I DROVE STRAIGHT HOME FROM WASHINGTON, D.C., because for forty-two of the last forty-eight days I had been away from my home. For seventeen days on the first trip and fifteen days on the second, I fasted. Maybe it was my feeble attempt to get God's attention. Please do not take my mention of fasting as bragging but instead as the sign of a desperate, struggling soul trying to find his way. Sensitivity to stories I had heard from people made me more tearful than I had ever been. This in itself was a big indicator that something had changed. Over the years I had done my salvation prayer many times. The problem was that total surrender never occurred. I wonder how many of my prayers actually were acknowledged by God. There is no question that I was not living a righteous life.

My failure to complete the self-imposed trifecta of interviews was humbling. For one, the goal I set was lofty, but more important, it was not God's goal. When it comes to serving God, one of the biggest misconceptions I had was concerning His will. The question I would always pose to God was, "What is your will for my life?" Just as I mentioned before, "for my life" does not belong in that phrase. What I did most of my life was create a very worldly exis-

tence and then try to shoehorn my life and stuff into God's
will. It never has worked and never will work. Most of you
reading this have never fully surrendered to Jesus and do not
even know what that really means. The final section of this
book is going to be more direct and is intended to encourage
you to look at yourself the way God looks at you. If you are
satisfied with playing on God's team for only a couple hours
a week, you are not on the team at all. The only one who
thinks you are is you. You are one of the millions who Jesus
tells, "I never knew you."

Ask yourself this question: "Why would this man reveal
such despicable behaviors of his life?" It is difficult to imagine that this self-deprecation could have any good outcome.
I love Jesus far more than I care about winning a popularity
contest, so being obedient is crucial. Your motives should
always be to bring glory to God's name. The complete essence of who you are should be totally surrendered to the
Lordship of Jesus Christ. When your motives are right, and
your heart is to serve, detecting God's will around you becomes much easier. Hopefully, the Holy Spirit is finished
prompting me to reveal the crud in my life, but if there is
something else brought to the surface that I am to report on,
you shall read it here.

I could not escape the stories I had heard from the hundreds of interviews. Praying for people in the many places I
went became common practice. My interest in watching
people increased significantly. Many times, my mind would
drift to what-if scenarios concerning people's lives. If I
sensed a troubled presence in someone, somehow, part of
that was transferred to me.

Was this the important characteristic that I had lacked so much all these years? Pride and ego had become a cancer destroying who I was. The treatment required high doses of empathy and compassion. In forty-two days, I talked to more people than I had in my entire life, at least on any meaningful level. God knew what He was doing all along. I tried to sidetrack my treatment plan by contacting a TV station and attempting to interview Obama, Trump and Clinton. Those plans were never part of the prescription. Things of the world became less and less interesting to me. The building that housed many unnecessary toys became a burden to walk through. What once was a place for show now became an embarrassment. My possessions were no longer trophies; they were evidence of a self-indulgent lifestyle.

When I finally realized that God looked at these items as an obstacle in my walk with Jesus, I knew what I had to do. Selling off the worldly accumulations would be systematic. The money was used for far better reasons. I am not sure if I can identify the exact moment when I realized it was not my stuff, but God's stuff. *Psalms 104:24 NKJV: "Oh Lord, how manifold are your works! In wisdom you have made them all. The earth is full of your possessions."*

The same compulsion that I had to buy excessively was now put into reverse. The more things I got rid of, the more things I wanted to get rid of, even some classic cars that I had for years. Everything was paid for, and we had the space to keep it. To most, that is all the justification you need, just as it was to me. After the Holy Spirit burns enough of the chaff out of your life, what remains begins to solidify. Now, you have a foundation that is much different from what it was before.

My family and the people around me were shocked at my behavior. For many years, I was the show-off out to impress everyone. They were all too familiar with my egocentric, excessive behavior, so most figured it was just a stage I was going through and there would be a change. The staggering thing about this was that for the previous twenty-five years or so, I was considered a "good Christian" man. Many of you could use the same fallacy that I did. You cannot have your cake (salvation) and eat it, too. In other words, you cannot be occupied with things of this world more than you are with the Kingdom of God.

For the next couple months, I spent nearly all day every day in God's Word, watching Christian videos on YouTube, praying to God, and searching. My wife and I were making small steps forward in our communication. My daughter was watching me very closely and would come to her mother's defense at the drop of a hat. Prior to my spiritual quest, I had a pretty good relationship with my daughter. Many times, we would go fishing together and enjoy each other's company. She loved turtles and frogs, just about any kind of pond life. Now, I felt that relationship was nearly severed.

Resentment toward my wife was welling up inside me. I held her responsible for turning my daughter against me. The reality was that I did it to myself. My wife's behavior and inclusion of my daughter in certain conversations was simply the fallout. The mismanagement of my role as spiritual leader, husband and father was the missile that caused the explosion. This, however, was part of the growth process when surrendering my will to God's. When we consider actions by others as a personal assault on ourselves, we are missing the point. Whether someone is a Christian or not, God could be using them.

Any time something concerning our character is brought to our attention, the first thing we should do is what? Find fault with the perpetrator? Make excuses for our wrongdoings? Blame somebody else? Deny our responsibility? Add a "but" anywhere in our response? If you have said any of these things, you are *guilty*. I have done every one of these and probably a dozen more. They are all wrong. The first thing we do is go to God and ask Him to reveal anything to us that we may be unaware of. You will find as you pour yourself out and allow Christ to dwell within you, your ability to be offended by others will constantly decrease. At this point in my journey, I was not yet getting a passing grade here.

God helped me increase my understanding. He removed almost all of my desires for things of this world. I accepted the fact that all that I have been blessed with was not for a lavish lifestyle, but to bring glory to the King. I was only partway there. The pride and ego issue had to be dealt with in a more complete way. I mention this briefly in Chapter 8, but now you will be able to see the picture more clearly. Each day, I would examine God's Word to see myself the way He does. One topic that caught my attention was remarriage. I had been married once before, and there is a great deal of controversy among Christians on this subject.

After several days of prayer and searching in the Bible, I felt as though I had no option. To prevent my wife and me from going to hell, I had to divorce her. A few months prior to this, I would have disregarded this notion as being foolish. The coaching staff had changed, and this was now a new ballgame. Every Scripture that I digested, I now took seriously, no matter how much indigestion it caused. Many people to this day would argue with me, saying that my conclusion was not wise. Of course, most of them have remarried. When you become completely surrendered to God, you should no longer consider other people's opinions that do not line up with what God has told you. Awareness of the Holy Spirit will rise to a point where you know what you need to do.

No matter how many YouTube videos I watched saying it was okay to remarry, I could not escape the anguish in my soul. I even talked to some pastor friends I had known for many years, and they did not believe I must get divorced. With my newfound awareness, these comments caused me to lose a lot of trust in their understanding. For three days, I wept and cried out to God. Why now? After all the changes I had made, what good could come of it? I could not understand after all that I had gone through what the purpose would be. Finally, on the fourth day, I told my wife. Amazingly, she took the news relatively well. Had we not been through so many rough waters, her response would have been much different.

She replied, "I do not feel that way, and I think we are fine, but I will leave it up to you." For the next three days, I continued down the same path. The burden on my soul was making it nearly impossible to stay above the waterline. I did not know how much more I could take before I sunk into the abyss. On the seventh day, God removed the burden from my heart. The weight that nearly drowned me in sorrow was gone. I floated back up to the presence of God, surrounded in a river of peace. Dwelling in His presence took on a new meaning. For the first time in my life, I understood the fear of the Lord.

The man who had patted himself on the back so many times for his achievements was now broken. I thought I had surrendered everything. God was fully aware of all the things that I sold and what I did with the money. But was I really at a point where I would forsake everything to follow Him? This was my Abraham moment. Would I sacrifice a marriage of twenty-eight years? Would I cause my sixteen-year-old daughter to have a broken home? The presence of the Lord had steadily grown within me. God wanted to know if I was going to be all in, or all out.

For whatever reason, God revealed Himself to me far more than He does to most. To this day I cannot understand why. There is absolutely nothing that makes me worthy of such loving treatment. The realization of the true piece of crap I really was made me love Him and fear Him to the point of obedience. As horrible as it would have been, I would have divorced my wife.

I want to explain the fear of the Lord a bit more. The word *fear* in itself conjures up the wrong kinds of images. I will try to reframe it in hope of providing a more suitable understanding.

The many despicable behaviors that God pointed out to me caused a paradigm shift. Thinking that I was basically a good guy was a roadblock to realistic understanding. The further down the list that God took me, the more I began to feel desperate for a Savior. As I compared the Word of God to myself, there was a considerable mismatch. My lifestyle was a mockery to what Jesus did on the cross. How dare I call myself a Christian and live the lifestyle that I did. Because of how much Jesus loves me, He showed me my fallen nature, and he continued to do so time and time again. The culmination of all my sin being stacked like cordwood made me realize how close I was to a fiery departure.

Through His great love and long-suffering, I came to a conclusion: Jesus is who He says He is, which means His words are true. His love is true. The consequences of rejecting Him are also true. Only by His demonstrating an unending love toward me was I able to have the correct understanding of the fear of the Lord. *Psalms 33:18–22 NKJV: "Behold, the eye of the Lord is on those who fear Him, and those who hope in His mercy, to deliver their soul from death, and to keep them alive in famine. Our soul waits for the Lord. He is our help and our shield. For our heart shall rejoice in Him, because we have trusted in His holy name. Let your mercy, O Lord, be upon us, just as we hope in you."* This awareness made it possible for me to see my pride, ego, stubbornness and disobedience the way God did.

The systematic dismantling accelerated. The layers had been so tightly packed that when one was removed another was right behind it, as with a Russian nesting doll. Many times I would think that I had reached a milestone only to have another doll revealed to me. Pride is baggage for many Christians. Almost all of us feel as though we have a corner on the market when it comes to understanding Scripture. We talk as though God gave us a personal letter, handwritten and addressed just to us. Several different scenarios were revealed to me before I understood I was also guilty.

When I understood what the fear of the Lord is, and that His Word is true, I started investigating. Constantly, I was probing my wife's understanding and my own of the Scripture. In many ways, she was far more advanced and had a naturally humble nature. As time went on, God aligned our walk more and more. Having confidence in my family's eternal destination became my top priority. My son's spiritual journey and mine were parallel in several ways but differed in others. He was never as materialistic as I was. He never had a profound need for flashy cars, helicopters and over-the-top everything. We had many conversations concerning God, and I felt confident that he was on a much better path than I was. But I was not too sure about my daughter. I began to ask her questions. At the time she was a junior in high school.

Her entire school career involved Christian private schooling. We attended a few different churches over the years, and she was involved with some of the youth groups. Through all my studying and Bible review, it became painfully clear that most churches were teaching an extremely watered-down version of the Scriptures, if not an outright deception. I am talking about principles that are spelled out clearly in the Bible. Was she a miraculous child whose life was initiated at a small Hawaiian church when people prayed? Yes. Did she have a Holy Spirit experience when she visited thirteen years later? Yes. Was she constantly being used by God to point out my prideful, ego-driven ways? Yes. Did she truly know what salvation through Jesus Christ meant? No.

When I realized and experienced fear of the Lord, I could no longer deny the Word. It says if we are truly obedient we must repent, stop sinning, finish the race, do His commandments, hear His voice, walk in the light, and love God with all your heart and mind, soul and strength.

With a new understanding of what the Bible really says about salvation, I laid it out for my daughter—not the phony little salvation prayer that many churches use, but the full-blown take-up-your-cross-and-follow-me exposé. Privately, my wife shared some concern that I may scare her off. As a family, we would watch several YouTube videos that I selected, then we would review Scripture to get a complete picture. Understanding that my daughter's eternal destination was at stake made this the top priority in my life. I questioned her about the teachings at the Christian school she attended. I wanted to blame them, but I could not. The responsibility fell squarely on my shoulders. If I had not been screwing around, pursuing everything in the world, I would have realized how crappy of a job I was doing.

The desperation I was feeling was like watching an explosive device count down to the last seconds. Every time my daughter left the house to go to school, I prayed for her safe return. The feeling of guilt was overwhelming at times. If she had got into an accident and died, I would have never forgiven myself. The fear of the Lord should give you an extreme sense of urgency, not only with your family members, but with all of humanity. Do you realize that someday we will all give an account for what we say, and what we did not say? How many people are going to end up in hell because you refused to share the Gospel with them?

I hope and pray that you take very seriously what I just said. My responsibility is going to be considerable. I misled many by offering people hope with a little salvation prayer and no substance, by presenting myself as a Christian in name only and not in my lifestyle, by not demonstrating love in all situations, and by not talking to someone about Jesus when the Holy Spirit had them ready to hear. Please, please take this very, very seriously.

I took a cautious approach with my daughter. In some respects, I know her better than she knows herself. She probably eclipses me when it comes to stubbornness. Jokingly I would tell her she is exactly like me except with different body parts. This gives me an advantage over my wife. My daughter's responses are similar to my own. Our thinking processes are rapid-fire, and we are quick to jump to conclusions. This poses a considerable problem. To hear the Holy Spirit, we have to slow down our response time. If we do not, then our conversations are primarily generated by the flesh and not by the Spirit.

Introducing new videos was a touchy proposition. Sometimes my daughter would accept them, and other times, she seemed completely uninterested. I was frustrated, but I knew I needed to be loving and kind and walk the talk. I wondered if some type of spiritual warfare was taking place. She seemed to be on edge and easily irritated. While she was at school, I looked into the subject in more detail. The fact that my wife and I were diligently pursuing a more Biblically based walk gave me concern. It may seem odd for me to have felt that way, but there was a reason why I did.

When we are worthless, so-called Christians, or just living in the world, Satan does not pay much attention to us. You are already in his camp, playing on his team. Upon detection of sincere obedience, he will rally some troops. Just like a pack of wolves, they will chase after the most vulnerable one in the herd. When the little girl calf does not have the protection of Jesus, she will become the target. What was about to happen with our daughter took us totally by surprise. Thank the Lord that He gave us the awareness that we needed prior to this event. This was not a situation for which you would want to be unprepared.

CHAPTER 17

WHEN I WAS CONTEMPLATING THIS NEXT CHAPTER, the Holy Spirit reminded me of something that I should tell you. I am going to share a story about something that happened many years ago. This was close to the time when God had me pray for the young girl who had a brain tumor. My faith was in the beginning stages, and I believe it was sincere. This was also a time when we were meeting with Pastor Rick and studying God's Word. I was in good soil and was sprouting up quickly. The problem came later on. Thorns of this world overtook the seedling that I was in my faith. As you experience the story with me, you will see how God gave me many warnings concerning my future.

My wife's teenage sister was staying with us for a few days during her summer break. Her sixteenth birthday fell during the days she was with us. I came up with the idea of renting a limo and taking everyone out to supper. Apparently, some big event was going on locally, because none of the limo companies had any cars available. The woman at one of the limo companies said she might know a driver who would be available. Within the hour she called back and said that a gentleman by the name of Buck could do it. The chain of events that led to his availability was remarkable.

After Buck picked us up, he drove my wife, her sister, and myself to a nearby city. As we were traveling down the highway, I began to have lofty thoughts. The windows were darkly tinted, so this would encourage people in other cars to stare as they passed. This was most likely the starting point of my pride, arrogance and ego. Jesus tried to reel in my fleshly emotions. Just a few minutes after the lofty thoughts had surfaced in my mind, another thought entered. If Jesus was here right now, what would he be riding in? At that instant, I turned my head to the left to view a beaten-up old VW beetle. The driver had long hair and a beard, reminiscent of how I pictured Jesus. He was beaming from ear to ear and did not seem to have a care in the world. While he was completing the pass, I abandoned my lofty thoughts and actually felt a bit guilty. I was bound and determined to make the best of it.

Our destination was thirty-five miles from our home. Buck the driver did not interact with us whatsoever. Once we arrived at the restaurant, Buck stayed with the limo. Still feeling guilty for my wrong thoughts, I asked the server to go out and take Buck's order and put it on my tab. We finished our meal and returned to the limo. I told my wife I was going to make the best of it and talk to Buck about Jesus. On the journey home, I positioned myself in the most forward seat. I told Buck I wanted to speak with him. He lowered the divider, and our conversation began. I was not prepared for what was about to be revealed.

Within a few minutes, Buck was telling me the details of his life, and they were worthy of a Stephen King novel. Several times he mentioned he did not know why he was telling me this. Even his fiancée, who he was going to marry in a few months, did not know the story. This was well before Facebook, YouTube, social media and all the other realities that people create. Some are true, and some are not. Buck was not trying to get likes or views or promote his beliefs. It was just one guy talking to another guy with the power of the Holy Spirit between them.

I asked Buck if he knew Jesus. He said he did, but something tragic had happened. Within the first few minutes of our conversation, he said he had made a deal with the devil. He traded his soul so that the devil would kill his father. Because I was a fairly new Christian and completely unprepared, I was nearly speechless. It became much, much more intense than this. Buck told me of his hellish childhood. When he was nine years old, his estranged father kidnapped him. He kept him hidden away in a trailer in the woods for nearly three years. Almost nightly, his father would come home drunk and molest him.

What he experienced was unbearable. He told me that he had learned the song "Jesus Loves Me" when he lived with his mother. Every night he would hide under the covers, praying that his father would not come home. As the tremors of fear shook through his body, he would sing the song about Jesus. He prayed that Jesus would end this nightmare. Hatred had consumed the innocence of his childhood. Anger and revenge worked in harmony to create a recipe for disaster.

When Buck was twelve years old, his mother found him and regained custody. For the next three years, Buck's shattered life was slowly rebuilt. He regained a small degree of hope, then tragedy struck again. His mother died, and having no other place to go, he was forced to live with his father once again. Buck's hatred toward his father had only increased. He began to pray to the devil to kill his father. He said he would turn over his soul if the devil ended the man's life. For nearly a year, he prayed for this every night.

During the time that Buck was away from his father, his father had stopped drinking. He started going to church and even professed to be a Christian. Buck never bought it and thought his father was full of s**t. Also, his father had remarried, and his new wife was a kindhearted Christian woman. One morning, Buck's stepmother came into his room hysterical. She said that she did not know if it was a dream or if it really happened. She told Buck how she had been wakened by the sound of her husband gasping for air and gurgling like he was suffocating. She said she felt an evil presence in the room and then saw a red mist hovering around her husband's neck. She prayed in the name of Jesus, and it disappeared.

Buck said, "She looked at me with great anxiety and demanded, 'Did you have anything to do with this?'" Buck said he replied, "Of course not." This date was etched in Buck's mind. When his stepmother left his room, complete and total terror overtook him. Satan had to be behind this, which meant Buck would have to be held to his end of the deal. The internal battle between the hatred he had for his father and the idea of selling his soul to the devil was ongoing. Several months later, the choking and coughing returned, and his father was diagnosed with throat cancer. Exactly a year to the day of the first visit by Satan, his father passed away. Buck told me that in the months before he died, his father apologized to him and asked for forgiveness.

"Maybe there was really something to the Jesus thing," Buck said. From sixteen to twenty-six, Buck's life was a living hell. The moment I met him, I knew something was off. Earlier in the evening, I could tell life was troubling him in a big way. He was chiseled, with mechanical expressions that seemed forced. Joyless and unhappy, he definitely appeared to be a troubled soul.

He then told me how he helped a friend clean out manure at a horse barn. They were using pitchforks. He said that it was all he could do to resist the temptation to plunge the pitchfork into his friend. He had visions of how the friend would slump over after the attack, what it would sound like when the tines of the pitchfork pierced his lungs, the wheezing sound that he would make as he gasped for air.

Buck said that almost everything he did revolved around killing himself or others. He then spoke about his urge to swerve into oncoming traffic, how it would it feel to crash, the crunching sounds the metal would make, what the bodies would look like lying in the mangled wreck. All the while, he was piloting a six-thousand-pound limousine, traveling seventy-five miles per hour down the highway. God knew even twenty-five years ago how strong-willed and stubborn I was. He put me in a potentially detrimental situation to see how I would respond.

Buck was beside himself. He knew he had made a deal with the devil. The ominous feeling of being trapped with no escape hitchhiked with him daily. I told him that only God could take back the territories in his mind and soul that he had surrendered to the devil. The words that I spoke to him did not come from my intellect. The Holy Spirit conducted the counseling session. At that time in my life, I was totally oblivious to the fact that God can speak through us. Not only that, when He is speaking through us, He is speaking to us. That was a great revelation for me. More on that later.

When we arrived at our house, Buck pleaded, "Can you pray for me right now?" We went into the apartment above the shop, and the four of us gathered together for prayer. My wife and I had been studying some material from *Basic Life Principles* and actually attended a seminar. Some of the material we reviewed concerned giving up ground. Most worldly endeavors and activities cause us to give ground to the devil in some way. Of course, I had done a horrible job of paying attention to these teachings. The ground that Buck had given up went way beyond anything I had knowledge of. Thank God the Holy Spirit gave me the words to say, because I was clueless.

I asked God if he would take back the ownership of Buck's soul, restore peace to his mind, set him free from all of the evil thoughts. "Please Lord," I prayed, "may the blood of Jesus cleanse Buck. He desperately wants to be forgiven for what he has done. Please show him your ways that he can find comfort in you. I ask in the name of Jesus that any bondage or evil control be broken."

Before I wrote this, I prayed that God would give me the words to say. I want to make sure I am conveying the situation accurately. There were more things that I prayed for, but this was the general construct of what I asked the

Father. This is the amazing part. The room was filled with the presence of the Holy Spirit. At the time, I did not realize what it was, but it seemed as though our senses and awareness were magnified tenfold. Each moment drifted by like a feather in the wind. Time was drawn out so we could experience the forcefulness of the situation. God responded!

Buck was a muscular man, with the build of a linebacker. I opened my eyes to look at him, and tears were streaming down his cheeks. The stress and strain that were locked in the muscles of his face had been released. He looked like a different person. He looked much softer, calmer. His first words were, "For the first time in ten years, my mind is clear." *2 Timothy 2:25–26 NKJV: "In humility correcting those who are in opposition, if God perhaps will grant them repentance, so that they may know the truth, and that they may come to their senses and escape the snare of the devil, having been taken captive by him to do his will."* We were all aware that something supernatural had happened. Even my wife's sixteen-year-old sister commented on how powerful it was. God had released Buck from ten years of torment.

This is what was so heartbreaking about the situation. My wife asked me several times afterward to contact Buck, but I was too busy with the cares of the world. I really had very little, if any, empathy or compassion for those outside of my family. I later realized that God had put me in a very powerful situation twenty-five years ago to learn, but I failed the test. I let Buck down by not following up. On top of that, the numerous individuals who I could have shared God's love with went by the wayside because of my selfish ways.

This story should be a stark reminder of the importance of serving others instead of ourselves. I pray that wherever Buck is today, he has a firm foundation in Jesus Christ. Some day we will answer for every person who God has appointed as our responsibility. We are to share the good news about the saving grace of Jesus Christ with the person at the grocery store, at the gas station, the doctor's office, the restaurant, sitting next to us in church—wherever and whenever the Holy Spirit prompts us.

I do not understand all the reasons why I was prompted so vividly concerning this event. There was not any room for misinterpretation, because I was supposed to share the story. The power of the enemy is real. We need to be prepared by absorbing God's Word at all times. *Psalms 119:11 NKJV: "Your word I have hidden in my heart, that I might not sin against you."* The desire to serve Jesus must consume us completely. Also, we need to be on alert constantly to avoid the fiery darts of the enemy. This statement leads appropriately into the next scenario that we will discuss, the internal choices of my daughter's eternal existence.

A sense of desperation about my daughter's eternity occupied my thoughts daily. For no particular reason, I watched many videos that revolved around demonic activity in people's lives. Because of the bad choices I had made and many doorways that I had opened in my life, I knew there was truth in much of what I watched. You may think it is a superstitious or fantasy world, but I guarantee that at some point in your life you will realize it is reality. On a Tuesday evening in March, my wife called my daughter downstairs for supper. When she came down, she told my wife to set the music level to number eight. She cannot stand silence and always likes some type of music in the background. My wife set the level at seven and rather than fiddling with the remote, she decided that was close enough.

Based on my daughter's response, you would have thought we had grounded her for a month. If looks could kill, as they say. The only interaction I had with my daughter that day prior to this was when I asked her if she was interested in watching a video. That probably translated in her mind to mean, "Dad wants me to watch another Christian video to 'fix' me." She had begrudgingly said she would watch the video if it was not too long. My wife and I were surprised by her reaction to the music. When we did our prayer for our meal, our daughter's malicious expression remained. She was like another person. She quickly finished her food and returned upstairs without speaking a word.

During the previous couple weeks, my daughter had tried to counsel a young man who was contemplating suicide. In addition to that, she was spending a lot of time with an old schoolmate who was a bit of a loner and probably suffering from depression. Having some understanding that demonic influence was more than a fairytale, I was concerned. She was going into enemy territory, and I did not feel as though she was prepared. I am not insinuating that either of these people was evil. Their actions, however, may have opened doorways to such influences. I am talking from personal experience here.

My wife and I talked briefly about the situation, expressing surprise. Normally, our daughter was a kindhearted, happy person. My wife went upstairs in hope of gaining some insight into the real cause for her behavior. I could tell the conversation was not proceeding smoothly. I walked up the steps and eavesdropped for a few minutes. My daughter was going on and on about Dad this and Dad that, mostly referring to my having it all figured out. That could not have been further from the truth. The recently minted understanding that the Holy Spirit had stamped out prevented me from reacting in an ego-protecting way. What was at stake was her eternal destination. Shame on me for all the times I let my ego and pride interfere with that in anybody's life. I calmly entered the room.

My daughter was lying on the bed facedown, her head buried in a pillow. She would not allow my wife to touch her. This was a first for sure. I had just spent the last three or four days watching videos and reading about demonic possession, oppression and influence. Whether you want to admit it or not, everyone has had this happen on some level. Here is the real shocker: It has even happened to so-called Christians. That is why the Bible says to put on the full armor of God. *Ephesians 6:10–12 NKJV: "Finally, my brethren, be strong in the Lord and in the power of his might. Put on the whole armor of God, that you may be able to stand against the wiles of the devil. For we do not wrestle against flesh and blood, but against principalities, against powers, against the rulers of the darkness of this age, against spiritual host of wickedness in the heavenly places."* You're living in a fairy tale if you don't believe this is true.

I started sharing with my daughter the concern I had regarding spiritual influence. I did not react to the negative comments she was making about me. Handling the situation with love was critically important. By mentioning how un-natural her behavior seemed, I initiated a reaction. She said, "It is hard to breathe," then she started coughing and shut-tered, "I feel like something is in me."

She continued to cough and gag, and my wife vigorously motioned for me to come over. My daughter had not watched any of the videos that I had, nor did I mention them. We both laid our hands on her and began praying. By the mighty name of Jesus, we commanded the spirit to leave. She continued coughing and spit up a small amount of foamy liquid. A few moments later, she was freed. She turned over, sat up, and with a huge smile said, "I feel better and so much lighter."

God had provided the perfect opportunity for our daughter to realize the importance of our Savior Jesus Christ. Nothing was fabricated or acted out, no special ef-fects or any other trickery. Undeniable truth is victorious every time. My wife had prayed with her to accept Jesus when she was five or six, but now was the time for the true plunge. We asked our daughter if she was willing to make a commitment. We were not talking about the phony baloney salvation prayer, but the full-on take-up-your-cross-and-fol-low-me commitment, with everything that's connected to it. She gladly agreed. God had to put an exclamation point on the situation. Had I not viewed it myself, I would have given a dozen other reasons why it happened.

My daughter now seemed happy and as light as a butter-fly, floating around on the breeze of her newfound love for Jesus. On her playlist, she had a Kanye West song called "Stronger." We were not aware that she listened to this type of music. She ran downstairs and said, "You are not going to believe this." Instead of that song playing for her, there was a different version. "Stronger" from Mandisa, with lyrics that were on the other end of the spectrum compared with those from the Kanye West song. But she had not put this song on her playlist, so it is difficult to come up with an explanation why it was there now. The real topper to the event was yet to come.

My wife led the local Moms in Prayer group. Because it took place the following morning, my wife was working on the lesson. She had copied three Bible verses to transfer to her handout paper. When she went to paste them, this phrase appeared: "We will do whatever we can to guide and encourage her." Word-for-word, that is exactly what appeared. I was in the other room when she came and got me. My first thought was that she had copied something previously and it was a shadow paste. After digging around a bit, I could come up with no reasonable explanation. Numerous unexplained things happened to me over the years, but still, I was a skeptic, always searching for an explanation. The fact is, God was continually moving around me, but unfortunately, I was blind to most of it.

A few months later, when the weather was warm, we had a wonderful family outing at a lake a short distance from our house. This was probably the most important thing a father can do with his daughter. Together my wife and I baptized our daughter. I felt as though God reached down from heaven that day and touched our family. The stage was continuing to be set for what God's will would reveal to us.

If you call yourself a Christian, and you are not experiencing spiritual warfare, there are probably a couple of reasons why you have not been tested. The big one is that you are doing nothing to advance the Kingdom of God, so why waste resources if you are already on the devil's team. The other one we will call the narrow gate. Your entire life is devoted to the service of the King. Rarely will an hour ago by that you do not think about Jesus. A day would never transpire without thoughts of your Savior. You love Jesus so much that you will tell anybody who listens. If you do not believe what I say about this, read the Bible. Why do you suppose there is only one story in the Bible regarding a servant of God being tormented by the devil? I do not know for sure, but I would say God rarely allows it. We can take comfort knowing that if we are being obedient, are surrendered, and have righteous motives we will enjoy His protection. Praise Jesus for His loving kindness.

CHAPTER 18

————

THE STRONGHOLD THAT THE THINGS OF THIS WORLD
had on me was finally broken. I was a lifelong inventor who
started building my first minibike before the age of ten. I
had helped build a hovercraft and always wanted to construct one with my own design. After many years of contemplating the design, I finalized my concept. I had the time,
space, shop and money for the project, but my desire had
vanished. The satisfaction I derived from inventing, which
kept my mind and body from a certain path of addiction,
had evaporated. Fortunately, my desire to learn how to become a better servant to the Lord had taken its position.

The Holy Spirit had to do a reality check with me just
to make sure. I had sold most of the items that I had bought
to impress people. They became a burden even to look at. I
still had the helicopter, but the excitement of owning it had
worn off months ago. I know we are not supposed to make
an oath, but I told God I wanted to give five hundred people
free rides. Remarkably, right at the five-hundred mark, I felt
the Holy Spirit was speaking to me. Here was what He said:
"You really want to be the cool guy who gives helicopter
rides, yeah?" Even though I had used the rides as opportuni-

ties to talk to people about God, I knew the Holy Spirit was right. I quickly surrendered and was content with putting it up for sale.

No matter how many times I tried to deceive God, I just was not smart enough to pull it off. He knew that in my heart there was only partial surrender of the helicopter. I was banking on the fact it would take a couple years to get rid of it. After all, that was how long it took to sell the last one. Ten days after listing it, the broker called and informed me that he had an interested party. They wanted to come out in the next few days to see it. I must tell you, in the first hour or so, I wrestled with God. "Seriously God? Ten days?" After about ninety minutes, I surrendered to the fact that I was a fool and asked God for forgiveness. A sense of freedom washed over me as one more item was checked off the list. When anything, I mean *anything,* in this world has a hold of you, you cannot completely serve Jesus. Period.

The larger struggle concerned our property and adventure activities. Since I had started the project without so much as a peep to God, I found myself flailing wildly in an ocean of ideas. I desperately wanted to do God's will, but I short-circuited the process from the beginning. If I had not been in the driver's seat, I could have relied on the best developer in the universe. Now, I found myself second-guessing everything that we were doing. Reacting quickly and being decisive in my decisions were hallmarks of my management style. When you fully surrender, those abilities must be used only when God clearly reveals His will. Otherwise, you are stepping back in and taking control.

The process of determining the direction of the facility

came to a near halt when I started enlisting my wife for suggestions. Decision-making caused her extreme anxiety, yet she would generally disagree with the directions I set. Our faithful staff had to weather the storm of our indecision. In my heart, I knew that somehow we needed to stir people to adopt selflessness as an admirable characteristic. Making a profit was never the intention. As we are struggling to understand how God would use the facility, He already had a plan. Several months later, we began to discover it.

The timeline of our life brought us to the point of traveling to the South. We met with my son and daughter-in-law, and they gave us the wonderful news about their pregnancy. They had hung a gift bag on the door handle of the house and had asked us to look in it before we came in. To our overwhelming joy, there was an ultrasound picture of a little baby. The frame around the picture was blue, indicating the gender. My wife and I were moved to tears, and our daughter was elated. Two and a half years before, they had suffered a very difficult miscarriage. There are many other layers to the story, including a few I touched on earlier. Most definitely, God had given us an awesome blessing.

My understanding of how God truly viewed me was sinking in. The humiliation that I experienced made me love Jesus even more. Character faults that had been nearly invisible were now coming into plain view. The introduction to a group of sincere followers of Jesus now became part of my lesson plan. God had orchestrated the connection to a lifelong neighbor who had surrendered completely to the Lordship of Jesus. He asked if we would be interested in joining their small group that met weekly. We decided to take him up on the offer. Recently, we had stopped attending the church where my daughter was involved in the youth group. All of the intense Bible study and prayer time were giving me a deeper understanding of God's Word. I started to compare what the pastor was saying to what God's Word was and came to the realization that there was a great chasm between what the pastor spoke and what the Word said.

When a person has tasted the authentic Word of God, anything substandard or counterfeit becomes unpalatable. A few weeks in a row, the pastor mentioned watching sports, TV series, and even zombie shows. Each depiction was flashing a red neon arrow toward hell. These But these diversions in themselves would not lead you there, unless they occupied the space that Jesus should. What once was considered good teaching now became repulsive, as God's Word shined a light on the true nature of what we were hearing. Satan has infiltrated the churches to such a degree that it is impossible to tell the difference between the church and the world. Many who sit in church each week do not even consider what Jesus instructed, but rather live their lives as they see fit. I participated in this practice for the majority of my adult life.

Our first encounter with my neighbor's prayer group revealed a collection of people who loved Jesus—who passionately loved Jesus. I had never before been with a group who could sit for three or four hours and discuss a handful of verses from the Bible. Not only that, no one dozed off, looked at their watch, or seemed uninterested for a moment. There was definitely something different about this group, and I wanted to discover more. The presence of some very

strong personalities made for interesting conversation. I
tried not to interject too much, so that I could gain a better
understanding of the participants. Some of the behavior
made me question whether it was cynical in nature.

Opposing views would be debated with vigor. Because I
was unfamiliar with the group, I thought that some of these
encounters were confrontational. The correct Hebrew names
of God and Jesus was a hotly contested subject. My wife and
I desperately sought God in prayer to help us understand.
We did not want any of our actions to dishonor God. If we
were to address God and Jesus in different names, then we
would gladly do so. Yeshua and Yahweh are some of the Hebrew names that were discussed for Jesus and God. For several weeks, we cried out to God for direction. No one ever
thought the name issue would prevent you from salvation.
Maybe there was a more correct and honoring way to address God.

Some of the debates and the constant revisiting of certain issues became troubling, mostly because there was still
pride in the self-righteousness of my personal beliefs. Several
times I wanted to stop going to the group's meeting. That
would have been a big mistake. The Holy Spirit revealed
many things to me through the group. I can imagine the
frustration the Holy Spirit has had with mankind. Paul talks
about the body of Christ having many different parts. How
can the different parts of the body function if Scripture does
not affect us in different ways?

The variations and insight should be cherished as a
broader understanding, not a cause of decisiveness that cre-
ates division and dissension. *1 Corinthians 12:11–14 NKJV:*

"But one and the same Spirit works all these things, distributing to each one individually as he wills. For as the body is one and has many members, but all the members of that one body, being many, are one body, so also is Christ. For by one Spirit we are all baptized into one body, whether Jews or Greeks, whether slaves or free and have all been made to drink into one Spirit. For in fact the body is not one member but many." We grieve the Holy Spirit by not being obedient to His promptings. There are two sides to that, but rarely do we give the second one any consideration.

The more apparent direction the Holy Spirit gives is a prompting to do something or a confirmation of something we are prayerfully considering. This is the big one we miss. If the Holy Spirit does not prompt us for a new understanding, we should leave it alone and move on. Here is what I mean: I took a deep dive into the proper names of Jesus and God. For several weeks, I researched Hebrew language and different Bible verses, and watched several YouTube videos on both sides of the discussion. I discovered legitimate arguments on both sides. I was not able to locate one video or Bible Scripture that indicated this was a salvation issue.

Finally, while walking in the woods one day, I fell to my knees and begged God to please clear up this issue for me. I have learned you cannot pull anything over on God. When you become fully surrendered and start serving with everything inside you, it is wonderful. He knew I had no skin in the game and that I did not have to be right or have to prove my point. I would gladly call Him whatever name the Holy Spirit led me to. I had this undeniable impression that told me, "If I am not prompting you, things must be okay. Move on." Immediately, it was resolved, and peace reigned supreme concerning this issue.

I suspect that many of the different denominations and church divisions occur because of our disobedience in situations such as this one. Strong-willed people are passionate about their beliefs. They may even be committed, obedient followers of Jesus who convince others that they have it figured out, and if someone really wants to be right with God, they should do what they do. Western civilization is running rampant. This kind of Simon Says mentality dominates instead of a Jesus Says mentality. Replace Simon with any of the modern-day prosperity-gospel preachers, and you will understand my drift.

What nearly became an exercise of my pride in spiritual matters instead became a greater love for my brothers and sisters in the Lord. Now when we get into spirited discussions, I marvel at the commitment and love that each member has for Jesus. I do not have to agree with every little point, and I do not expect people to agree with me on every point. That is the beautiful thing about being in the body of Christ: All the members have different functions, and we should celebrate each one because we need one another to function as a whole. The Holy Spirit revealed something else to me one day.

I was pondering my role of being a servant and realized how that was new territory for me. My mother had demonstrated service to the highest level, and my wife was pretty good as well. I did not have the excuse of not having good examples around me. I fell into a self-perpetuating lie that, because I was in charge, people were here to serve *me*. I had embraced the deception that I could be king of my own kingdom. A week or so prior to this, I had said to someone, "I want to have so much faith that if God says, 'Walk on water,' I would do that. And if God said, 'Go up to that person in the wheelchair and heal them in the name of Jesus,' I would do that." In my heart, my statement felt sincere and practical.

While mowing my lawn one day, I was contemplating what it meant to be a servant when this question arose: "So why is it you say, 'I will walk on water or heal the man in the wheelchair?'" The voice in my head sounded like the TV announcer from the *Price is Right*. The Holy Spirit amped up the description as if promoting a new product. Then I heard, in a normal tone, "Is there a reason you pick such lofty and high acts of faith? Why can you not be happy with sweeping the back room in my name where no one sees you?" Instantly, tears welled up and I repented. The Holy Spirit showed me a valuable lesson that day. The willingness to be a servant when no one knows or sees is the true sign of a servant's heart.

My wife and I continued meeting on Saturdays with our home church group. We would go from house to house every Saturday at 6 p.m. Rarely would our meetings end sooner than 9 p.m. One evening, they were held on Dearing Road, the same road that Pastor Rick lived on decades earlier. On our way home from the church group, we started reminiscing about our time with Pastor Rick. He was the pastor who discipled my wife and me at 7 o'clock on Wednesday mornings. We even babysat his children and greatly enjoyed them. His actions helped us focus where we should. Saying that he was a jokester would probably be an understatement. Rick loved setting up practical jokes. As time went on, I gave in to the desires of worldly pleasures, and we no longer stayed in contact with each other. Actually, I would have been embarrassed to be around him because I had so much hidden sin. Maybe that was why God kept us apart for so many years: He did not want Rick to experience another heartbreak of someone fallen by the wayside.

The last I knew, Pastor Rick was at a church less than two hours away from where we lived. Now that God had lifted the scales from my eyes, I understood things much differently. I even questioned whether Pastor Rick was preaching the truth. There was no reason to doubt that he was, but I had become much more skeptical due to an abundance of false teachings. I told my wife that, when we got home, I was going to see if there was a recent recorded message on the church website. In my heart, I hoped that Pastor Rick was still a God-fearing, truth-teaching, servant of the King. When I listened to the message, I was pleasantly reassured that he still taught the Bible as the ultimate truth.

That night, we made the decision to drive to his church the following morning. We really hoped that he would be there and we could renew our friendship. Not only was he there, but he also was available to have lunch with us after the service. Within a few minutes of the start of our conversation, the twenty-four-year absence of communication dissolved, and it was like old pals reuniting. The urgency to stir the churches in this country lie heavy on Rick's heart. Pastor Rick shared my concerns about the apathy, false teaching, rejecting of Jesus and many others. Almost instantly, we felt as though God had called us to a greater service. Somehow, we were supposed to be fighting the battle side-by-side.

God knew how much I needed good, solid people around me—I had willfully wasted nearly a quarter of a century! I never really had relationships with men who I could be transparent with and held accountable by. Around this same time, a gentleman started working with me. He was a mild-mannered, humble individual. Had I known how much I would grow to love this man, I would have had him start working with me much sooner. He possessed many handy-man skills. All the different equipment and projects that I was working on fit well into his wheelhouse of skills. Before long, we were praying together, sharing the struggles in our life, and enjoying each other's company.

The reality of understanding obedience to the King was starting to become clearer. In rapid-fire succession, very solid, committed servants to the King were coming into my life. The light that they shone into my life helped ignite the spirit reactor, bringing it to a critical mass. Now, there seemed to be an eternal fire burning inside me. The constant desire to learn more about Jesus and get closer to Him was a reality. Nothing else in the world seemed to matter anymore. Even mowing my lawn and working on the zip lines were burdensome. I had never really experienced God's will, because I was always looking in the wrong places. Mistakenly I had assumed that something was God's will for me, but it never was. Only when you become surrendered enough will God allow you to get close enough to the bullseye of His will to see where He is working.

Finally, I had relinquished enough control of my life that

I could start seeing things from an eternal perspective. My whole life had revolved around situations that I created, or at least thought I had. Many of them resulted in failure. Now opportunities were coming into play that were absolutely outside my realm of influence. Was it possible to move forward without having all the answers? Was it possible to go into uncharted territory without a map? Was it possible to trust everything to God? Was it possible not to be in charge regardless of the situation? God already knew the answers, but He wanted me to know.

CHAPTER 19

THE FACT THAT I NOW PROCLAIMED MY OBEDIENCE to Jesus left me both exhilarated and a bit fearful. *Psalms 56:3–4 NKJV: "Whenever I am afraid, I will trust in you. In God I will praise his word, and God I have put my trust, I will not fear."* Predictability is a sign of a self-controlled life, or at least the illusion of it. When we allow our lives to become so structured, we leave little room to see God's will. Pretty much everything that I tried to do in the name of God was not His will. Instead, it was my feeble attempt to offer my skills and expertise to God because He might "need" them. Hopefully, you detected a bit of sarcasm in that last remark. The reality is that most Christians make God fit their life instead of fitting their life to God's will. There is a threshold of surrender that one must reach.

Imagine a set of balance scales. You have a basket on each side. One is marked "Self-serving," and the other is marked "Surrender-self, obedient to Jesus." If you don't take enough out of the self-serving side, the scale will never tip in favor of obedience to Jesus. The great thing about the Holy Spirit is that He will show you the things you need to take out of the self-serving side. I believe a major transition occurs inside us at that tipping point. We don't have everything figured out at that point, but from then on, everything we do leans toward obedience to Jesus. This does not mean we are not vulnerable to tipping the scale back to self-serving. Fortunately, our ally is the empowering force of the Holy Spirit growing stronger and stronger within us. I hope that you all can experience the tipping point. Pursue surrender with a vengeance and reach that tipping point!

Even after I had spent a quarter-century acting in a self-serving manner and rejecting God, He loved me enough to give me a glimpse of His will. Once Pastor Rick and I were reunited, we contacted each other on a nearly daily basis. Rick shared some emails with me that he had received from a pastor in Africa. He was not sure how authentic they were. This was the first sign that God was revealing something to me that I had no control over. We decided to engage in conversation with the pastor from Africa. The email exchanges served three purposes. From the African pastor's side, they were intended to draw us in as a means of support. From our side, it was a fact-finding mission to understand how God may want us involved. The third and most important was that God was moving people into position so that our paths would intersect. He also wanted to see if we could pick up on the signs of where His will was working.

In the emails, the African pastor did not directly ask for money. Instead, he asked us to pray for his village because people were starving, did not have water, had died from typhoid, were experiencing severe drought, had no Bibles, needed seed and fertilizer, and had many other needs. In retrospect, I should have seen signs of deceit early on. The endearing terms the emails would use to describe our wives and other characteristics gave them the feel of being scripted. *Psalms 55:21 NKJV: "The words of his mouth were smoother than butter, but war was in his heart, his words were softer than oil, yet they were drawn swords."* But I was so enamored by the opportunity to help in Africa that I overlooked certain things. God would later reveal to me my errors. Some believers felt compelled to assist the African pastor and his village with their needs.

The initial sums of money were small by U.S. standards: a few hundred dollars. We would ask the pastor to show us how they used God's provision. He would share pictures and receipts. As time went on, we would ask about the cost of different needs that they had. At that point, he began to supply pricing for us. Then he requested that we visit, because he felt his people could learn many things from us. He claimed that the people of his village had listened to Pastor Rick's messages online. If this were true, they would have a baseline understanding of his teachings. I began a systematic question-and-answer through email. Eventually, we concluded that going to Africa would be prudent.

Because the rainy season was approaching, we had to either go soon or wait several months. Two months before Christmas, we made the decision to go. I reasoned that it must be God's will or I would not have become aware of the situation. Certainly, God is aware of my gung-ho attitude and anticipated I would react this way, so I did all the research on flight availability and timing. Once I had nailed down concrete facts, I contacted Rick. Because of his ongoing duties at the church, it would not be possible for him to make the trip. My wife was uneasy with the idea of my going to Africa alone. When I mentioned that Rick could not go, she said, "What about Josh?" Josh is Rick's son and a youth minister in Florida.

My wife's suggestion would end up having a monumental impact. I have learned to trust much more in her insights. There are a lot of moving parts to this Africa adventure, and I will pull them all together. Really, I should say God will reveal how they all fit together. Keep in mind that the tipping point leaning toward obedience to Jesus was in the rearview mirror by only half a dozen months or so. God has allowed me to have the funds and the time to do things quickly. This was only because I had accepted that they were God's funds and my remaining time on earth was for God. Now that my thinking had been recalibrated to eternal specifications, I was eager to be in God's will. I just was not quite sure yet how that all worked.

Who knows how far past the fifty-one percent tipping point I really was. Not far, I would say, because it was easy to slip back into old behaviors, even when they were disguised as doing a mission trip. I found myself boasting about how we were going to save the world starting with Africa. Did I ever speak those words? No, I did not. But somehow, I felt pride in my heart for what I was doing. I talked too much about it in our house church group. I gave more details than were necessary, and I made speculative predictions on what *I* was going to do. *Psalms 12:23 NKJV: "A prudent man conceals knowledge, but the heart of fools proclaims foolishness."* Any time I let my conversation drift into what-if scenarios, it might as well be labeled as foolishness.

Hopefully as I continue to absorb more of God's ways

through meditating on the Scripture, I will live them out. The day before our departure to Africa, we met with a couple who had started a youth ministry project eighteen years earlier. This was another situation where God connected the dots to allow an interaction to take place. A potential collaboration between our emerging organization and the youth ministry was definitely a possibility. I marveled at how quickly God was moving on multiple fronts. In my mind, it was hard to understand why there was such a radical change. As I pondered the tipping point and total surrender, it became clear. When any part of you tries to straddle the fence between living in the world and being obedient to Jesus, you are being only lukewarm.

I consider myself clever and able to debate with anyone. This arrogant, self-righteous opinion of myself even carried over to my relationship with God. Many of you are missing out on the relationship that Jesus wants to have with you. This is by your own choice, as it was mine. The reason that so many orchestrated opportunities are now happening in my life is because I fear the Lord, I love the Lord, and I am surrendered to the Lord. The Holy Spirit guides me to obey Him, and I quickly change direction when God indicates. And I search Scriptures to grow my relationship with Jesus on a daily basis. From a recovering pride-oholic, this may sound boastful, but that is not my intention. This is the reality of what changed in me. Remember, I am just over the fifty-one percent mark. The remaining days of my life and my obedience will determine how much that number changes. In my heart, I never want to revisit the actions of that disgusting person who God forgave.

It was going to take thirty hours to fly to Africa. That was hard to comprehend, because the longest I had ever been on a plane was around ten hours. Maintaining a civil behavior for triple that time seemed like an impossible challenge. I prayed that God would give me endurance and calmness in spirit so that I knew He was with me. Not only that, I was not representing myself anymore. Now more than ever, I was representing the Kingdom. The promotion to serve Jesus was something I took very seriously. Never in my life had I put that consideration first. My own comfort and care always outranked everything else.

Josh and I were blessed with an upgrade midway through our trip. During a layover, we met a missionary couple from Kenya and a Muslim woman and her daughter in a lounge designated for upgraded passengers. It seemed reasonable to think that God had orchestrated this encounter. Subsequently, all three adults became intertwined with our activities in many ways. The missionary couple became a viable resource for a later trip to Kenya. There is another little twist to this story, however. For whatever reason, my caring wife packed three bags of cough drops for me to take.

The husband in the missionary team had a cough, and the chances of us interacting would have been greatly reduced if I had not had the cough drops with me. I dug through my carry-on and offered an unopened bag to him. That is how our conversation was initiated, and he eventually gave me his contact information. I would not have thought those cough drops would have any significant value, but this is why God's ways are so much better than our own.

Gifts of the Holy Spirit are given on an as-needed basis.

To think that we have a permanent gift that God has granted us is wrong. This presumption can lead to our taking the glory instead of giving it to God. That is because we can believe it is our gift. Skills and abilities that God has allowed us to master in our earthly lives are often used in service of the King. I prayed that I would be able to understand or speak the native language when I was in Africa. Maybe next time I will, or maybe I never will. It does not matter, because I just want to serve the King. Over the years, I have honed my abilities to read people and discern the truth. That is where God wanted me to operate.

Through the many business deals and transactions that I was involved with, I developed a particular skill set. When I surrendered completely to the Lord, I told Him that I would exercise only the abilities that he called upon. What happened in Africa required me to use such abilities. I was resistant for several days, even though God was showing me something about a particular pastor. Finally, God prompted me to call a number on a receipt that was given to me, and it confirmed my suspicions. The pastor was deceitful in reporting the actual cost of items and was dishonest in other ways. I slept very little that entire night.

The ability to detect deception in others has manifested itself in me two ways. Being in a leadership role almost my entire adult life was one way. The second is in how much I deceived myself and God by being a make-believe Christian. Certain phraseology, facial expressions and body language tell a fairly complete story most of the time. The best way to determine someone's true motives is the discernment the Holy Spirit gives you. This is one thing you can always count on, but it is a gift. Do not make a definitive judgment in a situation unless you are sure the Holy Spirit has given you a word of knowledge. Always keep in mind that the Word of God stored up within you will give you guidance in most situations.

I was slow on the uptake, even though the Holy Spirit was nagging me to take action. This is a holy nagging I am talking about, not like your wife telling you to take out the garbage. All kidding aside, when you have a sense that is prompting you to do something, pay attention to it. I experienced this with increasing exuberance for a whole week. Had I been more attentive, we could have avoided a misstep that cost us a couple thousand dollars. Being able to walk close enough with God to see His will unfold in front of you is a magnificent thing. When you are surrendered and obedient, He does not let you stray far from the bullseye.

I believe the pastor from the African village was an honest man. He was unable to write, read or speak English. The friend of his that actually did the communication with us was also a pastor. He had been working with donors for years and had mastered the skill of deception. God made me aware of the little inconsistencies in his fabricated persona. Viewed independently, they could have been overlooked. When collectively considered, the evidence was overwhelming. By his own admission, he had written all of the email correspondences. There was no question he was an intelligent man, and I believe he thought he could outmaneuver us. If I had been operating with only my own abilities, he may have been successful. One of the many fantastic reasons to be totally surrendered to God is that you get supernatural help.

Earlier, I used the term the "bullseye of God's will." When we are surrendered, He gives us invitations to His party. There are many people on the guest list. We will encounter different ones throughout the event. God strategically mixes humanity together for multiple purposes. Ultimately, He wants us to see the bullseye of His will. It brings the maximum glory to His nature, which is love. Some of the individuals we encounter at the party may distract us from our goal. They may get us off topic or cause us to misplace our focus. Part of our responsibility in serving the King is to become aware of those individuals quickly and move on. If we remain close to Jesus, it will be easy to identify those who God has intended for us to be involved with. They may be the assistant manager at the hotel where you are staying.

That was exactly what we experienced on our trip. The most Godly, spirit-filled individual we met was right at the hotel. Not only that, he could speak English very well. We enlisted him as our interpreter and were able to weed through the deception of the one pastor. There is a very important lesson in this: *Do not let your objectives become unmovable.* That is an almost-guaranteed way to stray from God's will. As human beings, we are not nearly smart enough to comprehend all the moving pieces of God's plan. What He does want us to do is continue moving forward. *You ought to be in the Word and understand how clearly He makes much of His will easily known to us.*

When you are in the Word enough, in other words, *continuously,* you will see opportunities all around you to do His will. The problem most of us have is that we get it in our minds what we are to do, and that is what we go with. You will never hit the bullseye with that mentality. The man in Africa who God wanted us to meet was right at the hotel. This makes perfect sense in retrospect. For us to take any credit for identifying this individual would be complete deception. God orchestrated this encounter, so He will receive all the glory for the outcome. When we understand how much God loves us and that He wants the best results for our efforts, it is a marvelous thing.

Our goal should always be to resist drawing any attention to ourselves. If we are totally surrendered to God, He shows us a better way on a consistent basis. I have mentioned to friends and family how much I enjoy being corrected by God. There are many reasons for this, but it is primarily because His ways are always better than my ways. On top of that, it is a supreme demonstration of love for God to direct our path. *Proverbs 16:9 NKJV: "A man's heart plans his way, but the Lord directs his steps."* The closeness that we sense from His guidance is very compelling.

The lie of the devil is to hold on tightly to things that you have, to be in control of your own destiny, to have your own kingdom and be the god of it or create whatever gods you like. The joy and anticipation I experienced every day when I woke up in Africa were exhilarating. The feelings I got from the mountain of stuff that I had accumulated over my lifetime could not even compare. When I finally had the faith of a mustard seed, I was able to cast that mountain into the sea. What was revealed after the mountain of junk was gone was the opportunity to participate in God's will. It was my realization that loving others was far more satisfying than anything the world had to offer.

During our time in Africa, the young man who traveled with me preached several messages to the villagers. As he spoke, I assisted the locals in repairing several wells. God was okay with that because I was still operating in His will. The responsibility of being a truth detective became abundantly clear. The Holy Spirit had to prompt me a bit more in this area than should have been necessary. Hopefully in the future, I will be more assertive here. I had mentioned to a couple of people that if God wanted me to stay longer in Africa, I was willing to do so. In all the years that I have flown to different locations, I have never been bumped off of a flight.

When we went to board the plane, my travel partner, Josh, was checked in, and I was bumped. Almost instantaneously, I sensed that I was to stay longer. Through certain events over the next twelve hours, God confirmed His wishes. As the next ten days unfolded, many signs indicated that we should keep a lasting presence in Africa. Had I pursued my original plans, I could have missed many great opportunities that God laid out. The airline rescheduled me for the next day. When I arrived at the airport to see if I could delay my return by ten days, the airline was more than happy to oblige. That particular flight had been overbooked also. As compensation, I was given a free first-class upgrade for one of the legs of the flight.

Listening to God gave me numerous opportunities to continue in His will. Also, I was able to spend Christmas in another country with my newfound family. The young man who God had so masterfully placed in our path had a life-changing event occur on Christmas day. He had dreamed that his father had died, and in his dream, an angel came to him as he was standing by the grave. He was telling his father he loved him. The angel asked him, "Why did you not tell him when he was alive?" Neither the son or the father ever said the words "I love you" to the other. The young man was compelled to tell his father those three words on Christmas day. I was able to be a part of that and witness Jesus working in that household.

My wife and I enjoyed a completely different experience on this trip. We may have been separated by 8,320 miles, but we had unity in spirit. She chose to seek out opportunities to talk to people about Jesus. In fact, she even led a seventy-year-old man to surrender his life to the Lordship of Jesus Christ. With nearly every supernatural encounter that I had in Africa, she had a corresponding event in the States. We sensed the reality of what the Bible says. *Genesis 2:24 NKJV: "Therefore a man shall leave his father and mother and be joined to his wife, and they shall become one flesh."* I do not believe that we ever experienced the oneness on this level before. The dichotomy between this trip and my trip to Sarasota, Florida, exactly one year prior was staggering. Hurtful conversations of separation or divorce had clouded our desire for each other, largely due to my prideful and arrogant behavior. Now, God had restored us as a loving couple to participate in His will and bring glory to His name.

CHAPTER 20

────────

THE EXERCISE OF WRITING THIS BOOK HAS BEEN extremely helpful. The Holy Spirit is revealing to me that spoken words can easily be deceitful. It's more difficult to lie when the Holy Spirit sees the words through your eyes as you write them. There is a reason the Bible says the tongue can cause so many issues. *James 1:26 NKJV: "If anyone among you thinks he is religious (surrendered to Jesus) and does not bridle his tongue but deceives his own heart, this one's religion (surrender) is useless."* I added the words in parentheses to emphasize the importance of controlling what we say. Many things I have written about were painful and humiliating. The Holy Spirit and I went many rounds, but he always had the knockout punch. Ultimately, the thought "If you are going to be obedient, you will write this" would not depart from my mind and heart.

There is one more considerable secret that I have yet to reveal. I wrote the first six chapters of the book before telling anyone about it. My daughter, who just turned seventeen, edited the blog I wrote about the African journey. She found it to be enjoyable and was happy to tweak my clumsy way of writing. For quite some time, she has known that her spelling and grammar abilities exceed mine greatly. I had no intentions of her editing this material for obvious reasons, yet the Holy Spirit had different plans. The persistent prompting would not subside. Knowing how much God had stuck beside me all these years made me trust in His wisdom. Something about revealing the deep dark secrets in me would benefit her.

In my heart, I knew that God would somehow strengthen her walk with Him. If the cost was her losing respect for me because of my despicable actions, it was worth it. Many characteristics of our personalities are identical. God was aware of those characteristics in me twenty-five years ago. That is why He so plainly warned me of my stumbling blocks. First, it was with the vision in the castle. That was when the devil tried to take over me. The representation of his trying to sink back into me was my buying into the things of this world. At the point where the trend was reversed, I was nearly beyond salvation. After that vision, God revealed another outcome, if I chose the right path.

Sitting in the middle of a church service, I received my first Holy Spirit bear hug. I literally felt as though I would not survive the day, or even the next hour, if I did not go to the home of the girl who had a brain tumor to pray for her. This was God's movie trailer showing me what my future could be like. Instead, I hid the experience under a basket and told practically no one about it. *Luke 11:33 NKJV: "No one, when he has lit a lamp, puts it in a secret place or under a basket, but on a lampstand, that those who come in may see the light."* I had a wonderful opportunity to tell about the healing power of Jesus, however, I chose not to tell others of

God's glory. The Lord even went so far as placing me in the story of a man who was involved with gruesome intentions to harm others.

Nothing could have prepared me for the day that Buck, the limo driver, shared his story with me. Surrendering his soul to the devil to kill his father sounds unbelievable, yet this man had no reason to lie. He gave vivid descriptions regarding killing people. He fought battles daily to resist suicide. After praying for God to take back the territory he had surrendered to Satan, he underwent a physical transformation that was unexplainable. God had given me the perfect opportunity to exercise empathy and compassion. Instead, I continued on with my life without ever contacting Buck. Had I respected my wife's promptings and opinions, I would have listened to her urging me to call him.

I squandered three significant opportunities to grow in the Lord. Not only that, I was delivered from marijuana addiction by simply calling on the name of Jesus. Supernaturally, God enhanced my engineering abilities overnight. This may be hard to believe, but I can point to the exact year with matching documentation that shows a large upswing in our company's performance. This was achieved largely by developing our own specialized processes that still keep the company ultra-competitive today. All of this is because of God's blessing. Only a foolish man would not recognize what was right in front of his face.

My inability to react to God's cues resulted in my spending nearly a quarter of a century in a total wasteland. The long-suffering that God demonstrated in my case was unbelievable. He came to me in a potent way to give me one more chance. This just shows the true character of His enduring love. He basically spoon-fed me like a baby to turn toward Him. I will give a quick recap, so you can see how these incidents fit together. Looking back, I clearly see that I lacked empathy and compassion, so God inspired me to write some books that focus on becoming selfless. Before that, I was burned, rescued by a streak of light, and visited by the Authority of God. There were some immediate changes, but my pride and ego went pretty much unchecked.

My twenty-eight-year marriage nearly collapsed. Simultaneously, I was beginning to acquire empathy and compassion for others by interviewing hundreds of people. God had to resort to some extreme tactics because of my arrogant foolishness. The thing is, if I had not gone through those experiences, I never would have had the compassion in my heart to go to Africa. I thank God Almighty that He loved me enough to put me in these drastic circumstances. Otherwise, I would have wasted the remainder of my life thinking that I was going to heaven, when in reality, I was probably on my way to hell. I will never know for sure, because the burning desire to hang out with Jesus every day is all consuming. I talk to Him before I go to bed, first thing when I get up, and throughout the day.

Josh, who went to Africa with me to do evangelism, was God's prompting through my wife. He and his family moved into our home, or I should say God's home. Due to my disobedience to the Holy Spirit I created a situation that never should have existed. Josh and his family eventually moved out, but before they left I asked for forgiveness, and the restoration process is continuing. I firmly believe because of my issues with pride and the constant credit that people try to give, it is best that I do not live there, at least not most of the time. When you are committed to serving Jesus, God will reveal His will to you, and He will invite you to participate. God gives us resolutions to the situations we are involved in. We just have to pay attention closely and be fully surrendered to see them. Now I will tell you about a significant event that took place with my helicopter.

The annual aircraft inspection had just been completed, and my biannual flight review was also finished. I flew the aircraft home, and it functioned as it should. It developed an oil leak while sitting in the hangar, so I had the aircraft mechanic come out and take a look at it. We filled it up with oil and ran it, and it seemed to be okay. A few days later, oil began to drip again. I called the aircraft mechanic, and he said to fill it up with oil and fly it to him, so he could look into it further. I had a strange feeling, so a friend and I prayed over the helicopter. In the past, I always thanked Jesus after a safe helicopter ride. Obviously, I should have been praying before I went. This time I prayed, "God if we are not supposed to fly the helicopter to the repair facility, please give us an obvious sign."

We did some precautionary tests before we flew, but I still had a bad feeling. I told my friend I was going to fly it over the field and come back, then we would check it again. My friend rode with me, because she wanted a helicopter ride. Thank God we were flying only about twenty feet in the air when something happened. Instantly, we were sideways on the ground in a foot of snow. It felt like somebody had just pushed the helicopter right to the ground. The incident happened so quickly that it was hard to pinpoint the exact causes. We both walked away with only scratches, however, the helicopter was destroyed. This is something very interesting. I asked God to make it obvious if I was not supposed to fly the helicopter to the repair facility, which is located in a congested city. Also, an hour before the flight, I got a phone call from the number 888-444-0333. I am not into numerology and do not know much about it, but this particular sequence has a significant meaning. I tried to call the number back three or four times, and no one answered, but it did ring.

Anything I say about these numbers is not Biblically based, so I do not know if there is any credibility to it. Any repeating number in triplicate is said to be divine, just as the Trinity of God is divine. You can look up the meaning of these numbers yourself. Just keep in mind how God wanted me to purge myself of things in this world and to focus all my energy on bringing glory to Jesus. This means spreading the Gospel so that many will have the opportunity to be in heaven. The first two sets of numbers indicate change, new direction, God's safety, spiritual growth, and a number of other things. The one that is the most interesting for me is the last set of threes. We all know what zero means: nothing. My helicopter is a model 333. One hour before the helicopter crashed, did I get a warning? 0---333. If there is any meaning in those other numbers, then this is quite interesting.

My main mission with the helicopter was to give free rides, so I had a book in which I recorded each rider's name and experience. When I miraculously got my medical certificate after the seventh try, I made a deal with God. I did not take an oath or anything, but I said I would like to give five hundred free helicopter rides to show my appreciation for flying again. This may seem like an honorable gesture, but I was still trying to draw attention to myself. God convicted me in my heart regarding this, and that was why I agreed to put the helicopter up for sale. Here is the real interesting part: The woman accompanying me when the helicopter crashed may have been the 501st rider. I had logged roughly four hundred and fifty passengers in the book. There were several who rode twice, or were not recorded. I will never know for sure, but I believe the number of rides that I actually gave was right at that five-hundred mark.

Many people will think this seems like a stretch. But consider the number of times that God spared my life. If my other experiences had not occurred, my hypothesis would be vastly different. The last element to consider is my plan to move the helicopter to Africa. If it did not sell, I was going to consider it a sign from God that there was a purpose for it in Africa. I had already inquired about shipping it there. I will never figure out all the mysteries surrounding this incident, not in this existence, but I am sure that at some point I will get the whole story.

Most important was the prayer that we said and how clear God made it that I was not to fly the helicopter to the maintenance facility. I serve an awesome God who has my breaths numbered. I have mentioned only a few of the life-threatening situations in these pages. There are many more that I did not touch on. God's long-suffering and endless endurance to love is baffling. That is why I am so passionate about using my countless errors as a springboard for hope.

Jesus will take us in any condition we are and start the process of remaking us into his image. Please join me in this journey and get serious, because eternity is a very long time.

The next few pages are going to be worded in a very firm fashion. They are not intended to be a broad-stroke judgment call, but if you find yourself offended by what I say, you are likely *guilty*. Almost every time I was irritated by something Biblical used to point out my fault, I was guilty. During my unrepentant sin life, I figured God would give me a get-out-of-hell-free card for the occasional act of generosity. Anything I could use to justify my actions was fair play in my mind. I have been down that road so many times that I could drive it with my eyes closed. Man cannot manipulate God. You can try to be foolish like I was. *Galatians 6:7–9 NKJV: "Do not be deceived, God is not mocked; for whatever a man sows, that he will also reap. For he who sows to his flesh will of the flesh reap corruption, but he who sows to the spirit will of the Spirit reap everlasting life. And let us not grow weary while doing good, for in due season we shall reap if we do not lose heart."*

Many of you will not like the way that I plainly state what the Bible says. You will think that I am being condemning and judgmental, so I would like to give you a different understanding. I am assuming that most people who believe in God understand He has certain attributes. Here, I am not talking relational or emotional. These attributes I am referring to are more for dealing with the physical world. I think that we can all agree that God is the ultimate designer and engineer.

Human designers and engineers function with many of

the same parameters that God uses. On a daily basis, we design and engineer products with operational specifications. If the end product does not function to the intended specifications, the designer or engineer has every right to disqualify it from being used. The product may still perform to a certain level, but not as intended. The reality is, the designer and engineer want every unit to perform as designed. Why else would they put the time and effort into each one?

How can you compare a mindless product or machine with a sentient being? From a human perspective, you cannot. You also cannot compare human perspective to God's perspective. That is where the big rub comes in. We are not God. If we truly believe that God created the universe, then would you say His wisdom is so far beyond ours that we could be considered almost mindless compared to Him? Because of His great love for us, He gave us an opportunity to overcome specification deficiencies. Ultimately we have to accept the fact that He is the designer engineer, and He has every right to set the specifications.

I am not interested in winning a popularity contest or sugarcoating the Scripture. There are two things that are on my mind for anybody who reads this. Did I do my best to convey the truth of God's Word? Did I take the opportunity that God gave me on this earth to affect someone's eternal destination? I may never have the opportunity again to be used by God to influence your life and future.

I am going to look at only three verses. Each gives clear instruction about the type of actions that will keep you out of heaven. *Galatians 5:19–21 NKJV: "Now the works of the flesh are evident, which are: adultery, fornication, uncleanness,*

lewdness, idolatry, sorcery, hatred, contentions, jealousies, out-
burst of wrath, selfish ambitions, dissensions, heresies, envy,
murderers, drunkenness, revelries, and the like; of which I tell you
beforehand, just as I also told you in time past, that those who
practice such things will not inherit the kingdom of God."

Adultery. If you are having an affair with someone outside
of your marriage and are unrepentant and willfully sinning
and die this instant, *you will go to hell.* If you are divorced
and remarried, depending on the circumstance of your divorce
and the condition of your heart, you could be committing
willful adultery. If you automatically start justifying your
actions without consulting God, you are in *treacherous terri-*
tory. I cannot say definitively what to do because there are
variables. Never get divorced and you will not have to deal
with it.

Fornication. If you are living with someone and having
sexual interaction or just being sexually active outside of
marriage in a willful, unrepentant manner, and you die right
now, *you will go to hell.*

Idolatry. This is the one that is practiced by most Amer-
icans. Anything that takes your attention off of Jesus is idolatry. Most of my life has been centered on perfecting idolatry. That is a horrible skill. If you make an idol out of your
spouse, career, sports, entertainment, home, cars, boats, money,
success, power, being number one, self-pleasure, self-promotion or anything else besides Jesus, most likely *you will go to*
hell. Here is a crucial indicator for you to consider: If you are
offended by what I have written or think that I am totally
crazy, you are in quicksand and sinking fast. This is why your
first response should be, "God, if there is anything in my life

that is taking my focus off of You, please reveal it to me and I will get rid of it." Unwillingness to approach everything in our lives in this fashion is a strong indicator of not being totally surrendered.

The many different forms of idolatry will most likely be near the top of the list. The list I am referring to is the one containing the reasons Jesus says, "I did not know you." If he doesn't know you, *you will go to hell*. The majority of people who sit in church each week will fall into this category. Be honest with yourself right now. Is there something that you do not want to give up? Is there something that you quickly justify? Is there something that you spend hours and hours a week doing by choice? If so, then you give Jesus only the scraps. If you are fully surrendered to Jesus, the Holy Spirit will show you where you need to change. Please pray and do what the Holy Spirit is directing you to do. I am a chief offender in this area. That is why I am begging you to evaluate your life through God's eyes and make the necessary changes. Your eternal destination absolutely, positively depends on it.

Hatred, contentions, jealousies and outbursts of wrath fall into similar categories. If you have ongoing hatred toward someone, then you have not forgiven them for what offended you. The Bible clearly says if you do not forgive, you will not be forgiven. Do you create or encourage disputes, especially ones based on personal opinions or unsubstantiated beliefs? Is there someone you know at work, church or in your family, or an acquaintance who you are jealous of? They look better, make more money, have a more attractive spouse, their children are smarter or more athletic, everything seems to go their way, they have a nicer house, have nicer cars, they are a better Christian, or they are liked more by others. These are just a few examples of reasons for jealousy. Do you have outbursts of rage or uncontrolled angry responses to situations that happen in everyday life? Well, you might say that everyone does. There is a huge difference between actions and thoughts. Our thoughts should be submitted to the Holy Spirit for recalibration so that we act in a Godly way. If any of these behaviors describe you, and you are not repentant and think you are fine, then if you die now, *you will go to hell.*

I am telling you these details because I fear the Lord. The Bible says we should prayerfully take into consideration our every choice and ask the Holy Spirit to reveal the errors in our ways. Are you really willing to risk your eternal destination on anything but the truth of the Bible? Keep reminding yourself that the Design Engineer of the universe sets the specifications. You may not like it, but it is the reality of your reality. I could continue to describe how relevant every aspect of the Bible is. If you do not have the desire or motivation to find out for yourself, *you will go to hell.*

Much of my adult life has been a horrible waste of everything. Love, compassion and empathy were nearly nonexistent. Now that Jesus has shown me the real purpose of life, I want to share it with everyone I can. Although you may question my techniques of demonstrating love, I do so in a way that is straightforward and forceful. God put some very powerful lessons and invitations in my life. For twenty-five years, I put them on hold to pursue my own agenda. That was the worst mistake I made. The Holy Spirit has prompted me to be forthcoming about details of my life that I really do not want to share. I must believe that there is a purpose for this and that someone's life will be changed.

This process has led to a better relationship between my wife and me. My daughter, who edits for me, says that through what she has learned, she appreciates me more. The outcome from my admissions could have been detrimental. God is already showing there is a purpose for this, and where it goes from here is in the hands of others. I never could have told strangers, "I love you." I would have thought it was creepy and weird. After listening to many stories about people's lives and spending time in Africa with people who have nothing, I have changed. I never would have dreamed that I could tell people I loved them and mean it. That is what happens when you fully surrender to Jesus. He will show you how He loves.

When I tell you the next step, many of you may relate to the rich, young ruler. You could turn your back and walk away. Your career, house, cars, boats, closet full of clothes, bank accounts, 401(k)'s, sports and entertainment and hundreds of other earthly things will keep you from fully surrendering. Everything must be surrendered to Jesus. That is what it means to put Him first. If that means getting rid of all your earthly treasures to help the needy, then do it! God has revealed His will in a few different areas. I am willfully turning over what I stole from God. Those things never were ours, folks, and the quicker we realize that God owns everything, the better. Embrace the words of Jesus.

Here is a brief description to help keep our orbit close to His. Imagine Jesus Christ is our sun. He gives light, life and love. Our lives should orbit around Him. The closer our orbit is to Him, the more brilliant His presence becomes in our lives. As we get closer to Him, the gravitational force increases. With that increase, it becomes harder and harder to get away from His pull. Over time, that gravitational force draws our orbit in tighter and tighter. The meteors and asteroids are eliminated in those tight orbits around the sun. With the close orbit, we benefit from the protection and shelter from the fiery darts of the devil. The extra baggage of our planet (life) also is burned off and purified. Our goal as surrendered followers is to orbit as close to the Son of God as we can. Eventually, we will become one with Him when we are in His presence. Every time you look up at the sun, think of the Son of God and how close your orbit really is. *John 8:31b–32 NKJV: "If you abide in my Word, you are my disciples indeed. And you shall know the truth, and the truth shall make you free."*

CHAPTER 21

———

THE EARTH IS MY TRANSITION ZONE. WE MAKE many choices every day that tighten or loosen the world's grip on us. Picture, for a moment, a hot-air balloon. My spirit is the balloon, and the basket is sin. Our purpose is not to gently land on earth; it is to escape the gravitational pull of sin and return to our heavenly Father. Each time we cut one of the cords that restrict us from reaching our heavenly Father, we think that we ascend closer to heaven. But the truth is, we cannot cut the cords fast enough before others appear. The only way we can truly be set free is by one clean sweep that eliminates all the cords of sin simultaneously. There is only one way that can happen: through the redemptive power of what Jesus Christ did on the cross for us. The true born-again believer will operate under the guidance of the Holy Spirit for sincere and lasting change. There is another incredible aspect of Jesus that is almost always overlooked: His sacrifice was one of restoration.

Jesus wants to restore His children to their rightful place of a perfect creation without sin. The words that I wrote in the previous chapter are the reality of what the Word says, however, they present an insufficient picture of what Jesus does in our lives. We do not have to live condemned and feeling unworthy. *Romans 8:1–4, NKJV: "There is therefore now no condemnation to those who are in Christ Jesus, who do not walk according to the flesh, but according to the spirit. For the law of the Spirit of life in Christ Jesus has made me free from the law of sin and death. For what the law could not do in that it was weak through the flesh, God did by sending his own son in the likeness of sinful flesh, on account of sin: He condemned sin in the flesh, that the righteous requirement of the law might be fulfilled in us who do not walk according to the flesh but according to the spirit."*

We can come to Him totally enveloped in sins of the world. The process of sanctification will begin, and transformation will take place. That is how you will know that this is real. You will reflect on your old self and compare it with your new self and realize the growing disparity.

What once was a tiny space between who you are and who you were eventually becomes a wide chasm. Do not let stubbornness and disobedience hamper your transformation into something beautiful. Each morning when I wake up, I anticipate the overflowing love that Jesus will have for me. When we realize this truth in full, we become a conduit for love. Now love will flow through us from Jesus to others. When we completely abandon the concept of walking in the flesh, our spiritual potential is unleashed. The sacrifice that Jesus made on the cross for us takes on monumental importance. We can be in harmony with the Creator once again. Never allow the enemy to occupy any of your thoughts.

God has brought my understanding down a path of enjoying His love more fully. I no longer focus on past sin or potential future sin. Instead, I anticipate and enjoy the love showered upon me. This allows me to enjoy my relationship with Jesus and watch it grow. Each day becomes a mystery about how God is going to work in and around me. Our job is to step out in faith and discover the treasures of discipling others. We should be learning or teaching about Jesus each day. Many days we will do both. Often, our communication with God is most prevalent when we are talking to others about Him. I always try to evaluate the conversation I have with someone about God, because in the moments when the Holy Spirit is speaking through me, He is also speaking to me. Since I was given this revelation, the Lord has opened my eyes in many ways. Only when we become fully surrendered to Jesus are we able to walk in the fullness of that restoration process. *1 Peter 5:10–11, NKJV: "But may the God of all grace, who called us to his eternal glory by Christ Jesus, after you have suffered a while, perfect, establish, strengthen, and settle you. To him be the glory and the dominion forever and ever. Amen."*

Life takes on a totally different focus. Most of the things of this world become a burden, because they occupy my time and take away from time spent with my Savior. There is nothing more fulfilling than being in peaceful harmony with Jesus. When we finally get to the point where Jesus is first in our life, our spiritual understanding is unleashed; the deeper knowledge of what it means to be a spiritual being is revealed. In the process of sanctification, the Holy Spirit continues to refine us. The process is marvelous, and I am constantly looking for what God will reveal next. I love correction from the Lord. Obedience to His guidance draws me closer. A profound understanding has been revealed to me in recent events.

There is a reason why the Bible stresses the importance of dying to oneself. All external circumstances concerning the world should never affect the loving relationship we have with Jesus. This means we have surrendered our behavior to His lordship of love. When we start living in the fullness of His presence, it should become impossible for any person or situation to cause us to act in anything but love. This probably sounds quite lofty and optimistic—dare I say "unattainable." I would be the first to argue this point, using many examples of what the world can throw at you. What I once considered impossible in my own life has now become a possibility.

God has led me to Africa to establish pastor training and Bible distribution through Echo Africa. God has presented me with several difficult situations and provided me with ways to overcome them. He has used these situations to continue my training from the Holy Spirit. We wanted to purchase a used pickup truck to use in Malawi. A Malawi government official inspected the vehicle and gave us clearance to buy it. Because of all the corruption in the country, we thought this was a wise move. But after spending a considerable amount of money on the vehicle, we discovered that the VIN number had been tampered with. Because we are God's organization—Echo Africa came into existence because of His provision—we knew that we could not be involved with anything that was questionable. We went to the authorities with the information about the VIN number and were told that we could keep the vehicle. Tony, the executive director of Echo Africa, made a profound statement: "Maybe God wanted us to buy it so that it could be returned to the rightful owner." He was, in fact, speaking prophetically.

Through extensive investigation, we learned that the vehicle was stolen from South Africa. Thank God we were diligent in our pursuit of the truth. Also, we had put new tires on the truck and repaired the transmission. Normally a situation like this would really bother me. We would have no way to recoup the money we had spent. The guy who sold us the truck had moved and could not be reached. The police informed us that he was involved in many other suspicious vehicle sales. Because of the huge duty placed on vehicles in Malawi, a four-door Ford pickup can cost more than $70,000. We paid less than half that for the used one. Now, the rightful owner would be getting back his vehicle in better shape than it was when we bought it, but here comes the most interesting part.

Joel, the person who sold us the vehicle, professed to be a Christian. In fact, he had been a pastor at one point. On top of that, he expressed great interest in what Echo Africa was doing. The day we met, he wore a leather bracelet that displayed the words "I love Jesus." I asked him where he got it, and he said, "South Africa." Then he took off the bracelet and gave it to me. I really liked it and wore it often.

For several months we were in limbo concerning the truck. One day, I looked down at the bracelet and thought, "I am not going to wear this anymore." It was a constant reminder of the guy who had ripped us off. The Holy Spirit quickly reminded me, "What does that have to do with wearing a bracelet that says, 'I love Jesus'? In fact, I want you to continue to wear it and pray for Joel." Amazingly, I quickly accepted those instructions.

The bracelet has become a symbol of the restoration process in my life. It also reminds me that Jesus loves everyone and wants us to pray for those who may have done something against us. The old me would never have been able to accept this. By the Holy Spirit that lives within me, all things are possible. *Matthew 19:26 NKJV: "Jesus looked at them and said to them, 'With men this is impossible, but with God all things are possible.'"* I am in Africa now as I write this final chapter. By the end of the year, when this book comes out, I will have spent nearly twenty weeks here. This is just the beginning of what God wants me to do. The blessing of loving people far outweighs anything the world has to offer.

You may be wondering about the name of the book, and even the cross on the cover. Let me tell you about the cross first. I was inspired by the Holy Spirit to fold a $5 bill into the shape of a cross. When the bill is folded properly, "In God we trust" appears front and center on one side of the cross. My wife, daughter and I, plus a few close friends, hand out folded $5 bills as a witnessing tool. Satan once used a love of money to draw me away from God. Now God uses it to draw people closer to Him. In addition, we spend time in the villages in Africa. I love being around the children and playing games with them. Many of them did not know what a high-five is. Through the prompting of the Holy Spirit, I told them it means you are "all-in" for Jesus. Now, thousands of children in Africa are doing high-fives as a way to honor Jesus. Here is one more additional fact about the $5 cross.

The great emancipator, Abraham Lincoln, is on the $5

bill. He was key in abolishing slavery. He also initiated the National Day of Prayer. His 1865 proclamation to establish that day is profound. Everyone should read it and think of the situation in our country today. We are falling apart as a nation, and you can easily trace the rapid decline back to the point when prayer was eliminated from schools. Time is short, and we cannot deviate from the Word of God. Look closely at the $5 cross. The one on the cover has been altered. Instead of saying, "In God We Trust," it says, "In God I Trust." Only by the power of the Holy Spirit can such transformations happen within an individual.

Now to the title. After the visitation, and the years that followed, I believed the title of the book, should I ever write it, had to be *How to Piss Off God*. Many of the Pharisee types will not even read it because of the title. But the title must stay, and here is why. My perception of God has changed. As I experienced a deeper and deeper love, I came to realize that I had never pissed off God. But it was my personal journey to reach that understanding. I fully and completely believed it for several years. Through the loving kindness of the Holy Spirit, my perception has changed. What I thought was extreme disgust with me was something else.

What I experienced was God's unending love to restore the proper relationship with me. Because of my great disobedience, hardened heart, and prideful existence, drastic measures were necessary. Only by His drastic love could I be drastically changed. This statement resonates deeply in my soul. As I write these words, tears stream down my cheeks. The Spirit of God is confirming within me the Great Love that exists. In my timeline and spiritual journey, both thoughts exist together. They are separated by what I thought and what I think now. God knew that through this process I would realize He was never pissed off at me. Instead, He drastically loved me. He knew in the end that I would respond to His love. In the end it is always through His love that restoration will draw us to Him. *Isaiah 55: 8–9 NKJV: "My thoughts are not your thoughts, nor are your ways my ways, says the Lord. For as the heavens are higher than the earth, so are my ways higher than your ways, and my thoughts than your thoughts."* God's ways of loving us are far greater than we can fathom. His love may take on unfamiliar characteristics that we may not associate with love. In the end, though, we will always realize it is love.

When the Holy Spirit confirmed in my heart to publish this story, the name was confirmed. The reality is that this story is about a transformation process. My understanding as a man is that *How to Piss Off God* has been transformed into thoughts from God: *How to Accept Love from God.* You see, we may not like the form that His love takes, but God knows what it takes to form us into His image.

ABOUT THE AUTHORS

Chris Salow is first and foremost a surrendered servant and friend of Jesus Christ. He insists that all glory, honor, and praise belongs to Jesus. Because of God's grace and mercy, he was allowed to be an accomplished inventor, machinist, CEO, and novelist writing under a pen name. A life-changing accident and spiritual awakening inspired him to share the messages of humanity, hope, and redemption he has received. God prompted him with this: "If you are completely truthful about yourself, I will use you to speak my truth to others."

Maria Salow is his daughter. A linguistics student at Cedarville University, Maria witnessed and participated in Chris's transformation process. God prompted Chris to have Maria edit this book. She is eternally part of the story as it continues to unfold.

Made in the USA
Monee, IL
14 September 2023

42557142R00152